The politics of socialism

Themes in the Social Sciences

The politics of socialism

An essay in political theory

JOHN DUNN

Fellow of King's College, and Reader in Politics
University of Cambridge

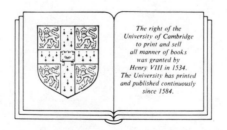

The right of the
University of Cambridge
to print and sell
all manner of books
was granted by
Henry VIII in 1534.
The University has printed
and published continuously
since 1584.

CAMBRIDGE UNIVERSITY PRESS

Cambridge
London   New York   New Rochelle
Melbourne   Sydney

Published by the Press Syndicate of the University of Cambridge
The Pitt Building, Trumpington Street, Cambridge CB2 1RP
32 East 57th Street, New York, NY 10022, USA
296 Beaconsfield Parade, Middle Park, Melbourne 3206, Australia

First published 1984

Printed in Great Britain at the University Press, Cambridge

Library of Congress catalogue card number: 84-7110

British Library Cataloguing in Publication Data

Dunn, John, 1940–
The politics of socialism.—(Themes in the
social sciences)
1. Socialism
I. Title   II. Series
335   HX73

ISBN 0 521 26736 6
ISBN 0 521 31840 8 Pbk

Contents

Analytical table of contents

1 SOCIALISM AS POLITICAL THEORY

I.

The subject of the book: an account of the emergence, intermittent advance and recent faltering of socialism in advanced capitalist societies. Three demands on any political theory. First, realism over the character of existing political and social orders: requires understanding both of actual consequences secured and counterfactual consequences averted. Socialist thought attends more carefully to actual than to counterfactual consequences. (Conservative thought does the reverse.) To offer a defensible politics for advanced capitalist societies, socialism must correct this imbalance.

II.

Second, to capture a coherent and convincing conception of human social good. Socialism can offer powerful criticism of capitalist production in these terms. Advantages promised by socialism. Doubts about the coherence and moral adequacy of these promised advantages. Weakness of existing socialist accounts of the social good. Need for a cogent conception of social equality. Undesirability of developing a socialist conception of the good in detachment from the practicalities of political action.

III.

Third, to indicate how to make the best of our historical social opportunities. Much the most important aspect of any serious theory of politics.

IV.

Doubts about socialism today in relation to all three demands, especially in relation to third demand. Discouraging lessons of the period of transition to socialism.

V.

Problem of transition. Does the revolutionary road to socialism ensure the construction of tyrannies? Must the reformist road within capitalist democracies always be blocked by resistance from defenders of private capital?

VI.

Is a transition to socialism actually possible at all?

VII.

The 1983 British General Election as an object lesson in socialist failure.

VIII.

Allocating responsibility for outcomes of democratic processes within capitalist (or other) societies. Despite manifestly unfair terms of political competition in capitalist democracies, most failure in this is deserved. (It does not follow that success within it is deserved.)

IX.

Persisting internal contradictions within the political project of British social° democracy. The British working class in no sense a hegemonic class.

X.

Political parties as agencies of representation. Tensions between socialist conceptions of the social good and the requirements of political action.

XI.

Socialist political representation: trustworthiness and efficacy. Revolutionary politics as locus of peculiarly painful collision between these requirements.

XII.

Party and class: social identity, class interest and institutions for the defence of such interest. Tensions between these. Parties as relatively weak shapers of social identity.

XIII.

Subjectivity of social identity. Ecological changes in the context of working-class identity. Political claims to the allegiance of an industrial working class never a matter of ascription. No external epistemic standard for human social identity. Political identification as the conferring of trust.

XIV.

Determining the political interests of a class. Organizational requirements for serving such interests effectively.

XV.

Liberal and authoritarian models for socialist political parties. Premises of the liberal model; individual assessment of interests and institutional economizing on trust. Superiority of liberal democratic models as learning devices. Indefensibility of socialist authoritarianism.

XVI.

Interpretation of class interests as basis for the right to rule: cognitive adequacy, social identification, competitive efficacy.

2 DEMOCRATIC SOCIALISM AS A POLITICAL PRACTICE

XVII.

Learning and refusing to learn from political experience of socialism. Presumed advantages and questionable achievements of socialism in rationalizing production.

XVIII.

Socialism as a critique of the capitalist mode of production. Limitations of socialist productive rationality as a practical restraint on further socialization of advanced capitalist economies.

XIX.

Pressures towards socialism within capitalist societies. Class consciousness and social experience. Political consequences of this consciousness and experience in advanced capitalist societies: impetus and resistance. Varieties of European social democracy. Dependence for any benign transition to socialism on democratic forms of action. Political instability of commitment to more radical versions of democracy.

XX.

Determinants of the balance of political pressures towards socialism in an advanced capitalist society. Pressures towards a restoration or deepening of market relations. Recent failures in socialist politics.

XXI.

Aversive pressures towards socialism in advanced capitalist society unlikely to diminish in near future. Aversive pressures away from socialist expedients only modifiable by an increase in causal understanding.

XXII.

Objective setting of socialist politics; domestic distribution within an international system of production. Political opportunity for a socialist restoration of economic efficiency. Absence in Britain at present of any political entity capable of taking this opportunity.

XXIII.

Subjective setting of socialist politics: culture. Importance of culture in the political articulation of aversion towards capitalist production. Unintended consequences of post-war socialist politics in Britain.

XXIV.

Comparative simplicity of culturally expressive socialism and difficulties of reconstituting efficient economies on a socialist basis. Potentiality for cultural revulsion from capitalist ownership inseparable from the latter. Difficulties in transposing such revulsion into effective political action.

XXV.

Extent of socialist transformation always determined by political struggle. Political struggle always potentially violent. Struggle for hegemony as a struggle for rational trust. Indispensability of trust to a defensible socialist polity. Hazardousness of socialist political promises: attempts at cultural reconstitution. Instrumentalism and ingenuousness in socialist politics.

XXVI.

Ideological strength of capitalist democracy. Difficulties of combining socialist government with political freedom.

XXVII.

Socialism as the reimposition of cultural values upon economic processes. Accident-proneness of socialist governments as ground for the indispensability of political liberty. Undemocratic socialism as pure menace.

3 'TRUE SOCIALISM'?

XXVIII.

Modern socialism as critical and utopian rather than constructive. Indispensability of a convincing account of realizing socialist political intentions.

XXIX.

'True Socialism' as unsullied by historical experience.

XXX.

Utopian socialism as rigorous moral thought and as indolent wish-fulfilment.

XXXI.

Assessing the causal coherence of socialist conceptions of the good. Possibility that cultural values might rule: peaceful transitions to socialism and the reformability of post-revolutionary socialist parties.

XXXII.

Political power under True Socialism. Socialism committed, willy-nilly, to greater trust in political power than is needed in capitalist societies. Inadequacy of the project of synthesizing a wholly transparent society. Markets and rational central planning. Implications of the economic experience of existing socialist states for the economics of True Socialism: problems of socialist economic planning.

XXXIII.

Pattern conceptions of social good and their limitations as a charter for socialist political action.

4 MORAL

XXXIV.

Aligning social and political institutions with moral intuitions: socialism as response to the systematic offensiveness of capitalist society.

XXXV.

Advantages of capitalist democracy as a setting in which to improve the intellectual and political coherence of socialism. Necessity of developing a more honest and adequate socialist conception of political organization and action. Capitalist democracy as a safeguard against socialist authoritarianism.

XXXVI.

Intellectual causes of socialist political failure.

XXXVII.

Capitalist democracy as natural political form for a society aware of its inability to resolve its own contradictions.

FOR BIANCA

Preface

Why do any human beings choose to be socialists? Why has socialist politics proved in practice so frequently disappointing? How far can socialist ideas still serve to inform and guide political judgement in modern states for the better? Are the evident weaknesses of socialist politics in all its varieties likely to lead to its disappearance from modern political activity in the readily imaginable future?

Politics is an attempt by creatures of limited understanding, skill and virtue to reshape the societies in which they live their lives. Political theory is a more or less systematic attempt to assess the meaning of these activities and their prospects for success. The purpose of this essay is to focus more clearly the significance and the prospects of socialist political activities in wealthy capitalist societies. It neglects many issues which are importantly relevant to thinking about these questions: the present state and prospective future of the capitalist world economy, the immense variations in social and economic structures between different capitalist countries,[1] the distinctive historical experiences which have shaped socialist politics in different societies in Europe,[2] North America, the Far East and the Antipodes, the political and economic history of countries which have experienced major anti-capitalist revolutions in the twentieth century. All of these are important considerations in their own right and all have some real bearing on the issues

---

[1] Much of the modern historiography and still more of the sociological analysis of capitalist societies is directly concerned with the attempt to analyse these variations and assess their implications for political consciousness and action. See particularly the development of British Marxist historiography by E.P. Thompson, Eric Hobsbawm, John Foster and Gareth Stedman Jones and the criticisms which this has elicited from non-Marxist historians. For a very interesting, if highly dogmatic, account of these structures in a very different advanced capitalist society see Rob Steven, *Classes in Contemporary Japan*, Cambridge University Press, Cambridge 1983.

[2] For a convenient presentation of aspects of this experience from a variety of angles in twentieth-century France see, for example, Tony Judt, *La Reconstruction du parti socialiste 1921–1926*, Presses de la Fondation Nationale des Sciences Politiques, Paris 1976, and *Socialism in Provence 1871–1914: a Study in the Origins of the Modern French Left*, Cambridge University Press, Cambridge 1979; R.W. Johnson, *The Long March of the French Left*, Macmillan & Co, London 1981.

considered here. But even the best informed of opinion about them could not be a substitute for what is attempted in this essay.

The two questions which are considered here can both be expressed very simply. What explains the political attractions of socialism in advanced capitalist societies? Can socialist politics still constitute a rational and civilizing form of political enterprise in these countries? The answer to the first question presumed here is unoriginal to a degree: that the more clearly visible capitalist ownership relations come to be in any modern society, the less plausible they become as sources of moral entitlement to material goods, and the more confused and unstable the material conditions for the majority of the population which follow from them, the less easy it is to protect them through the use of state power in a representative democracy. The answer to the second question is considerably less clear but perhaps a trifle more original. It is at present an eminently practical question in Great Britain, France, Spain, Italy, Sweden and Greece. If the answer to the first question is even broadly correct, it might in the longer run become an eminently practical question in any advanced capitalist society, even ones like the United States or Japan in which the historical presence of any form of socialist politics at a national level has always been pretty muted. It is this second question which the book as a whole is principally intended to address.

To discuss the immediate practical prospects for socialism in Britain with any adequacy would require a close consideration of, amongst other matters, the history of class relations and class consciousness in the country, of the problems of economic policy posed by the highly distinctive features of the British economy and of the intricacies of electoral geography and party organization. But all of these together could do little to illuminate the question of whether socialist political agency can still reasonably expect to prove, on balance, politically benign in practice in this or other countries over any length of time. If it cannot reasonably expect to prove so, whatever short-term political success it achieves will be necessarily ephemeral. The theoretical problems of socialist politics are not specific to a particular society, merely to particular types of society. This essay considers the politics of socialism in advanced capitalist societies whose political order, in most cases, at present takes the form of a representative democracy. Socialism is concerned with many other matters besides the exercise of state power, but it is politically puerile to ignore the centrality to socialist politics of the struggle to acquire, and to exercise state power for what are hoped to be good ends. In political theory socialism must be defined in the first instance in terms of the exercise of state power and the organization of an economy; it cannot simply be dissolved into the name for an assemblage of miscellaneous cultural enthusiasms which happen to be current at a particular time. The classic questions of socialist political theory concern the form of the state and the organization of the economy.

These questions certainly require to be supplemented in many different ways (for example by questions of gender and cultural formation). But supplementation cannot serve in lieu of an answer. Since the 1840s Marxist vocabulary and conceptual apparatus has proved systematically disingenuous over questions of political action. But it has also sustained the most serious attempt to understand and express the occasions for there being any socialist politics at all. At present, this combination of evasion, debility and insight has left modern socialists with no coherent and defensible concept of the desirable form for a socialist state, and with an increasingly indefensible set of presumptions about the appropriate organization for a socialist economy. The representative democracies of advanced capitalism are highly imperfect state forms, but as a political order they are all too clearly still superior to anything yet fashioned to compete with them. Much of the residual viability of capitalist societies in the face of recession depends directly upon this plain and effectively publicized superiority. But it is above all the incoherence of modern socialist economics which threatens the political prospects of socialism in wealthy capitalist countries. The main point on which this essay insists is the political frivolity of any socialist politics which fails to face and to surmount this challenge. The grounds for taking this grim view are provided by the increasingly clearly understood failures of socialist economic planning when put into practice. This is a complicated and technical subject and not one on which political theorists are equipped to pronounce. I have drawn extensively on two thoughtful and sympathetic recent treatments of these issues by Alec Nove and Michael Ellman, both leading experts on the modern Soviet economy, who cannot plausibly be suspected of gratuitous hostility towards the USSR. The implications of their work are all too clear and they are strongly confirmed by the much wider range of historical and analytical work referred to in the accompanying annotation.[3] Unless socialists can solve intellectually the problems which this body of work has identified, their future political activities are overwhelmingly likely to be either futile or inadvertently destructive.

Socialism is a political theory (or a diffuse family of political theories) on which hundreds of millions of human beings in the present century have tried to act. There is every reason to expect the future history of capitalist production to continue to spawn such political enmities. What really matters about socialism in the long run is whether it can be made into at all an

[3] The history of the modern Soviet economy, and to a lesser extent of the economies of Hungary, Poland and other Eastern European 'socialist' countries is now extremely well understood. The more theoretical writings of Brus, Kornai and many others have made considerable progress in assessing the implications of this experience. For a convenient introductory survey of these implications see Michael Ellman, 'Changing Views on Central Economic Planning 1958–1983', *ACES Bulletin, XXV*, 1 Spring 1983, 11–29, and at greater length Alec Nove, *The Economics of Feasible Socialism*, Allen & Unwin, London 1982 and Michael Ellman, *Socialist Planning*, Cambridge University Press, Cambridge 1979.

adequate political theory, and whether it possesses the intrinsic intellectual and moral resources to guide political action for the better. What is certain is that unless the historical world created by modern capitalism, and by socialist political agency in response to this, comes to be understood rather better than we yet understand it, the chances of changing it for the better are remarkably slim.

In the last few years the views set out here have been shaped and reshaped constantly by the experience of teaching and conversation with my colleagues at King's College and the Social and Political Sciences Committee of Cambridge University. Paul Ginsborg, John Barber, Geoffrey Hawthorn, Istvan Hont and Gareth Stedman Jones, for one reason or another, will approve of rather little of what is expressed here. But, however involuntarily, they have taught me to see these questions the way I do and I am deeply grateful for the stimulus, the intellectual seriousness, the patience and the good fellowship with which they have done so. I am especially grateful to Istvan Hont who, since he has been at King's, has taught me by his intellectual rigour and passion far more about socialism and its travails than I was at all willing to learn. I have been helped seriously once more in preparing the essay by my friends Patricia Williams and Geoffrey Hawthorn. I owe a particular debt of gratitude to Giuseppe and Luciana Fontana for their generosity in making it possible for me to live and write in peace in their house in Vedasco with its ravishing views over Lago Maggiore.

Socialism as political theory

I.

What political theory attempts to grasp is, as Charles Taylor puts it, 'what is going on, what is really happening in society'.[1] This essay is concerned with the political theory of socialism: with what has really been happening in the emergence, the protracted advance and the recent faltering of socialist politics. It considers this question principally in relation to the experience of the wealthier and more advanced capitalist countries of Europe, America, the Antipodes and the Far East, assuming, with Marx,[2] that the superiority of socialist civilization, if it is to be established at all, must be so by its greater capacity to resolve the practical problems of those societies which are materially the most advanced.

There are three demands which it is reasonable to make of a political theory: the first is that it should capture what political structures, political institutions and political relations are actually like at present – what they consist in, what they prevent and what they bring about (the simplest understanding of Taylor's formula). The second is that it should capture our sense of how we might coherently and justifiably desire any human society to be. The third is that it should tell us what is to be done to realize in practice as intrinsically desirable a social and political condition as can in fact be realized and sustained in the historical circumstances in which we find ourselves.

The first requirement, however, is a good deal more exigent than it may at first appear, since no representation of political structures and institutions can claim to capture what these consist in and amount to at present without assessing what they are now, in each particular setting, preventing or bringing about. And no assessment of what political institutions or structures in a particular setting are now preventing or bringing about can hope to be both clear and decisive without a complementary assessment of why exactly the main features of the society in question are as they are. To capture the meaning of political structures and institutions for a particular society at a particular time is therefore also to identify the degree of responsibility that political choice and its concomitant coercion have for the existing character of human social relations. To identify the responsibility of political choice for what it brings about is a delicate exercise in historical analysis, usually in practice to be conducted on grossly insufficient evidence and as a matter of some practical urgency. But hasty and speculative though this assessment is virtually compelled to be, it is hard to imagine anyone seriously disputing its indispensability in politics. To appraise such responsibility effectively requires a deft and steady judgement; but to see the need for this appraisal requires only the merest common sense.

It is perhaps less clear on initial consideration that political appraisal necessarily requires an assessment of what political choice is in fact responsible for preventing. And it is certainly far less clear how exactly to attempt to assess responsibility for what has not occurred than it is to do so for what already has.

Political causation logically involves the same apparatus of hypothetical and counterfactual conditionals as natural causation. We cannot explain in politics why things are as they are unless we can specify clearly what factors under what circumstances would render them different in what ways. To assess responsibility for what political choices have brought about or are bringing about involves a close attention to the intentions of political agents. It is such intentions, in the last instance, that are central to any adequate account of why these agents have acted as they have done or are acting as they are doing: not because they are sufficient by themselves to provide this explanation, but because they define precisely what there is to explain. But even an assessment of what political choices are at present bringing about must involve far more than the intentions of political agents, since so much of what happens in politics happens in ways and for reasons which no particular political agent intends. In the assessment of what political choices have prevented or are preventing the intentions of political agents play a still more modest role. Here intentions indicate merely what the agents in question had in mind in acting as they acted, whereas most of what they have in fact excluded or prevented from occurring by these particular actions is likely never to have been considered by them.

Other things being equal, human agents are more uncontentiously responsible for what they intend to bring about than they are for the unintended consequences of their intended actions. But in politics this asymmetry possesses far less weight than it does in purely private conduct.[3] The accurate assignment of blame is central to the practice of representative and responsible government[4] − and equally essential to the appraisal of unrepresentative and irresponsible government, enlightened or otherwise. But the blame which it is necessary to assign for these purposes is blame for consequences rather than for intentions. Despite the implications of political rhetoric, malevolence on the part of rulers is a less frequent and on the whole a less acute menace in politics than is the inadvertent promotion of policies which are practically disastrous. (It is so even today for roughly the reasons suggested by Machiavelli and Hobbes – that even the worst intentioned of sane rulers has good prudential reason to govern in most respects and for most of the time as beneficially as he or she can. It is puerile to assume that Mr Chernenko or Mrs Thatcher or General Jaruzelski or President Reagan actually *intend* to cause massive harm.)

As with other expressions of human intention, political choices certainly deserve praise or blame, both in themselves and for the light which they throw upon the beliefs and dispositions of those who make them. But the form of appraisal which they most insistently require is not an appraisal of the ethical sensibilities of those who make them, but rather one of their consequences for the full range of human beings whom they affect. Political proposals in relatively stable political societies characteristically take the form of a promise to extend an existing range of professed good intentions and seldom or never advocate a gratuitous abridgement of a range of currently valued goods. It is hard for even the most scrupulous and discerning of political leaders to assess the compatibility and interdependencies between political goods, and unattractive to all but the most scrupulous to acknowledge the full extent of the potential clashes between them. One of the commonest forms of political miscalculation, both deliberate and inadvertent, is to add to the schedule of intended or promised political goods without subtracting accurately from this schedule the other existing political goods, the preservation of which will be or would be precluded by realizing the promised novelties.

The most damaging suspicion about socialism, at least in advanced capitalist societies, is that it rests, in good or bad faith, on just such an error in social and political book-keeping: that it assumes the possibility of retaining all or most of the advantages of these societies from the viewpoint of most of their inhabitants, while firmly removing a number of features which most of their inhabitants cordially and justifiably detest. This suspicion might, in principle, be confined to social and political theorists, but it is a matter of major political importance that it has in fact been quite effectively extended, through news media and educational institutions, to a considerable proportion of the population of advanced capitalist societies. In the face of this extension, any form of socialist politics in such countries which does not elect to be both dogmatically arrogant and brutally adventurist must set itself to confront this suspicion and to dissipate it, if it can in fact be dissipated, by rational means.

Can there be a coherent and defensible socialist politics for advanced capitalist societies, or is any such politics irretrievably disingenuous or confused?

II.

The second demand that it is reasonable to make of a political theory is that it should capture our sense of how we might coherently and justifiably desire any human society, or at the least our own society, to be. In this aspect a political theory is simply one component of an overall conception of the human good or right, of what is intrinsically desirable or justifiable. In the face of capitalist societies at all phases of their history, it is in this respect that socialists have consistently found it easiest to muster and retain a confidence in the superiority of socialism.

To see capitalist societies as just societies it is necessary to conceive production and exchange within them as free transactions between independent individual persons, and to see the private appropriation and voluntary transfer of natural goods and cultural artefacts as morally unproblematic. Neither of these representations of the working of a capitalist economy or the character of capitalist property relations is comprehensively at odds with the entire history of capitalism. But the former gives a ludicrously selective and distorted picture of how modern capitalist economies, domestic and international, determine what is produced and by whom; and the latter, despite Robert Nozick's argument,[5] has no plausible connection whatever with the actual private holdings of property in any contemporary capitalist society.

The moral rationalization of capitalist societies, in David Hume[6] as in Friedrich von Hayek,[7] involves the deliberate endorsement of a complex range of consciously artificial practices, the workings of which are explicitly recognized to be often at odds with our unreflective and spontaneous moral sentiments, and to require systematic practical defence and ideological buffering against the interferences of the latter. The artificial virtues and rights which a capitalist society requires are to be defended, in Hume's eyes as in those of Hayek, because of the beneficial consequences of their regular operation, not because of their intrinsic moral charm. It is true that in the initial attempts to defend them systematically, capitalist production could be presented more plausibly as a set of free transactions between independent individuals than would be possible today. In particular, the system of property holdings of the society which preceded capitalism had come to appear even more arbitrary and disjoined from social or economic function than the distribution of 'entitlements' of modern capitalist societies at present appears to the majority of their inhabitants. Market exchange itself, likewise, appeared more unequivocally as an instance of free action when seen in contrast with the miscellaneous assemblage of monopolies, privileges and restraints on production or trade that was characteristic of most of eighteenth-century Europe, or with its extensive residues of dependent or unfree labour.[8]

4

Socialist critics of capitalist production have promised a wide variety of improvements on the experience of its operations: the restoration of production for use rather than exchange; the retention of freedom of labour without the attendant threats of the labour market or unemployment; a suspension (by some means or other) of the culturally blighting or psychically alienating effects of an extended division of labour; the production of a greater abundance of material goods (with or without a marked abatement in human greed and a pronounced improvement in human taste); a sharp diminution in the waste of resources and the destruction of human habitats; the systematic and planned use of human productive powers and skills and the full weighting of externalities in all productive and distributive decisions; the return to a more intimate and human scale of productive organization; a drastic diminution (and eventual disappearance) of the role of coercion in organizing production and exchange and in guaranteeing mutual security; the emergence of relations between men and women (and perhaps between adults and children) which are no longer inequitable and psychically deforming; the establishment and maintenance of distributive justice or of a condition which, because of its categorical transcendence of scarcity, renders distributive justice otiose.

And so on.

Not all of these goods are plausibly consistent with each other even in logic; and even those which are are evidently likely on occasion to militate against one another in practice. Some categories are conspicuously absent from these lists which have been of great ideological importance in human history thus far and which remain of urgent significance to most human beings in their own lives today: most notably, that of personal merit or desert. (This omission is a characteristic which modern socialist conceptions of justice share with those of liberals like John Rawls or, perhaps, Ronald Dworkin.)[9] This particular absence may well be of some political importance. The promise of a form of society in which merit will no longer be urgently needed and desert no longer be seriously appraised is likely to stir the suspicions of even the more credulous. Is the territory in question, the destination projected, not perhaps the land of Cockaigne? And even if it offered a more reassuring description of a prospective destination, there would be some doubt how far this conception succeeds in registering the distaste for many of the features of capitalist society which is actually felt by most of its inhabitants. Simply in terms of social justice it has always been (and emphatically remains) one of the most evocative complaints against capitalist society that in practice it distributes privileges and opportunities in a manner so weakly related to human merit.

But waiving the question of the logical consistency, practical compatibility and comprehensiveness of the set of goods included in the socialist prospectus, this list raises two obvious doubts. The second of these must be postponed for the moment. (Even on the bewilderingly optimistic assumption of the logical consistency, practical compatibility and comprehensiveness of the socialist conception of the good, what grounds are there for expecting it to prove realizable in practice?) But the first doubt is genuinely a question about the conception of the good itself. Is the socialist conception of the good both coherent and morally adequate simply as a conception of the good? This is not, mercifully, a question which it is necessary to pursue here; and it is certainly at present a topic on which it is intellectually prudent to be agnostic. Socialist thinkers have in fact been extremely unimpressive in the urgency and pertinacity with which they have attempted to explore and expound their conception of the good. Both the strengths and the weaknesses of liberal conceptions of the good are much easier to assess following the efforts of John Rawls and his critics.[10] Nothing comparable is available as an exposition of a socialist conception. In its absence the suspicion that socialist conceptions of the good may be irretrievably equivocal in content and opportunistic in expression remains very much alive.

As characteristically set out, the socialist conception of the good amounts to an inventory of possible objects of desire in the ordering of social, economic and political relations. All of those listed, more or less cursorily, are of course not merely possible objects of desire but putative goods actually desired by at least some persons in most advanced capitalist societies (even, for example, the United States of America). Insofar as they are in fact logically consistent with one another it would, other things being equal, be perfectly reasonable to hope that they constitute not merely a coherent conception of what is intrinsically desirable but one which can be given a systematic moral defence. (It is an important aspect of the modern liberal conception of the social and political good, with its insistence on the priority of justice, that it begins from the question of how a set of human social relations could be given a systematic moral defence.) But while it would be perfectly reasonable to hope this, it would not, without further close inspection, be at all reasonable to expect it. An inventory of miscellaneously assembled desiderata in social relations, compiled simply by the conjunction of more or less widely conceived and expressed social discontents, stands every chance of containing a multiplicity of contradictions. Given the diversity of men's social situations and the idiosyncracy of their temperaments, it would be little short of miraculous if such a conception proved to offer a clear, stable and authoritative extra-historical standard for the appraisal of all human practices.

Such scepticism does not, of course, afford any reason to distrust the force of particular socialist enthusiasms or aversions. But it does suggest the importance of taking these and assessing their force one by one and refusing to presume that they enjoy any guaranteed moral or practical affinity for one another, let alone any guaranteed causal relation to the future history of human society. There are, therefore, serious grounds for doubting, first, the unity and determinacy of the socialist conception of the good, secondly its internal consistency and the practical compatibility of its various components and thirdly the prospects of its being realized in practice.

As a particular instance of these doubts, we may consider briefly the value of equality. It is virtually a truism that socialist conceptions of the good diverge from liberal conceptions, not merely in laying greater emphasis than the former on social solidarity and the virtue of fraternity, but in laying somewhat less stress upon the value of liberty and considerably more stress on the value of equality. All liberal political theories, perhaps indeed all political theories which embrace in any form the legacy of the Enlightenment, acknowledge the merits of some forms of human equality: in particular the equal enjoyment of civil rights, or equality before the law. Likewise, democratic forms of liberalism accept equality of political citizenship amongst adult members of a community as a criterion of full political legitimacy in a society. But socialist political theories seek, with more or less zeal and rigour, to extend the scope of personal equality from legal and political relations to the entire domain of social relations. Of course, it is the case that some versions of liberalism, notably those advanced by Rawls and Dworkin, also place very substantial weight upon the value of equality, seeing it, for example, as a necessary condition for justice in social relations that the conception of the good of each human agent be accorded equal weight in shaping the organization of the society to which he or she happens to belong. But it remains the case that those who choose to identify themselves as socialists are apt to do so in large part because they attach particular weight to the value of equality, and that those who find themselves most keenly hostile towards socialism are apt to do so because of the intensity of their aversion to what they see as the follies and dangers of egalitarianism.

Some forms of egalitarianism certainly are silly, objectionable and hazardous. A society which insisted on regarding all its members with equal respect and patience irrespective of the character of their actions would not be so much deplorable as simply incomprehensible – it would also be extremely short-lived. Any real society requires effort and restraint of its members; and the actual members of any real society will vary dramatically both in their capacity for restraint or effort and in the use which they elect to make of these capacities.[11] It might in principle be possible to obliterate esteem in a particular society for athletic or aesthetic prowess, for cheerfulness or moral dependability, for political zeal or educational dedication, for energy or love, for courage or modesty. At their worst, Russia during the Terror, parts of Eastern Europe at times since 1945, Germany under Hitler, Kampuchea under Pol Pot, may have gone some distance towards attaining such a goal. But whatever bearing such episodes may be

7

thought to have on the merits of socialism (and only the very sanguine or dishonest would presume that they have literally no bearing at all), what they bear on is hardly the socialist conception of the good, of what is intrinsically desirable. No well-considered conception of human good could rest on the fatuous belief that real human beings are in fact equal in their claims on each other's respect or admiration, or that practically they could be caused to become so, or that a society in which, *per impossibile*, they had been caused to become so, would for that reason be a good society. To recognize all other conscious human beings as bearers of human consciousness, and all other human beings broadly capable of choosing their own actions as free agents, is a requirement of justice in relations between persons. But it serves no good purpose to describe such recognition (or the forms of mutual treatment which appropriately emerge from it) as the according of an equality of respect. Respect is a real and relatively infrequent emotional orientation of one human being towards another. We could not and should not respect one another equally. (How, knowing what I know about myself, could I respect myself in the same sense and with similar sentiments to those which I feel towards another person whom I genuinely do *respect*?)

What is respected in a particular society at a particular time may well be (perhaps characteristically has been and is) open to strong moral or aesthetic objection. But to criticize the values of a particular society, even where these are especially competitive in character, is not to advance the claims of equality. A society which set little store by athletic prowess or mathematical skill in comparison with political zeal or mutual human warmth would leave ample scope for the expression of human inequalities and probably, indeed, for the display of human competitiveness. Such competition might or might not represent in practice a clear moral or aesthetic improvement. (Athletic or educational competition are not always very edifying; but neither, for that matter, is the systematic reward of hypocrisy. A society which genuinely values political zeal will in practice encourage the insincere miming of political zeal at least as effectively as it will its authentic display. And once it has contrived to do so, human mimetic skills being as unequal as they are, it will find it infernally difficult to distinguish the real from the feigned.)

Where the value of equality does play a major and a more cogent role in specifying a socialist conception of the good is not as the overall goal of social organization. Rather, it is in the systematic criticism of arbitrariness in the distribution of social, economic or political advantages. In this context, as the trajectory of western political and social theory since the sixteenth century makes very evident, egalitarian principles possess considerable critical power. The demand for justification in terms of right or contribution has been levelled against one feature after another of the feudal political, economic and social order of late medieval Europe and one feature after another has duly succumbed to its ideological impetus. The main brunt of the attack has fallen upon the possession of privileges which cannot plausibly be represented as earned by the efforts or attainments of their possessor: privileges of political choice,[12] or social status[13] or inherited wealth. In the case of political choice or social status there is no clear residual distinction between liberal and socialist conceptions of the good. Indeed liberal theorists like Rawls and Dworkin no longer show much active desire to distinguish themselves from socialists even over the issue of inherited wealth. Rawls's principles of social choice, for example, involve treating the productive capacities of all members of a society as a collective good and adopting distributive policies which guarantee that these capacities contribute to the maximum to the needs of those who, in comparison with their fellow citizens and fellow productive agents, will profit least from their membership of the society. Even liberal justice, when rigorously explored, proves able to sanction only those forms of economic inequality which can validly be justified to every citizen of the just society. (The main residual distinction between the views of Rawls or Nozick and a socialist conception of the good arises over their – plainly contingent – assumption that substantial material incentives are likely to remain a precondition for energetic and effective productive activity, and over their firm refusal to society as a whole (or to its government in particular) of the authority to press conceptions of the good upon recalcitrant individual citizens. This contrast between socialist and modern liberal conceptions is not in any sense frivolous. Indeed the first is sufficiently cogent to merit the closest consideration from any optimistic socialist, while the second, if it perhaps precludes a very coherent liberal conception of public education, certainly registers a legitimate occasion for acute political anxiety.)

But, in contrast with liberalism at least, socialism is principally a doctrine about the political implications of economic organization. The political lines between liberal and socialist conceptions of the good, accordingly, are best drawn over more specifically economic issues. From this point of view, Robert Nozick's insistence that Rawlsian justice frequently involves the treatment of adult economic agents as means rather than ends, that it requires the prohibition of capitalist acts between consenting adults and interferes systematically with men's or women's right to give what belongs to them to others whom they wish to benefit, gives a much better sense of the nature of liberal objections to socialism.[14] Nozick, of course, can only sustain such claims because he is incautious enough to offer – what Rawls very prudently withholds – an account of legitimate appropriation, of how human beings can become entitled to material goods and how, accordingly, it is possible to distinguish categorically what does belong to a particular person from what emphatically does not. Nozick's account has not impressed his critics.[15] Indeed, it is not clear that it impresses even Nozick himself. But it is important to note, as the author himself does,[16] that it is not necessarily any easier to justify a right of collective appropriation for a particular human collectivity (perhaps the people of Kuwait) than it is a right of individual appropriation. Taken as a whole, Nozick's work reinforces two important points: first, that there remains an intimate link between the defence of capitalist property relations and the defence of individual freedom of action in economic affairs; and secondly, that socialist criticism of capitalist property relations is more safely grounded in a vigorous scepticism over the moral status of all human appropriation than it is in the more or less dogmatic affirmation of collective property rights in the assets of a single society at a particular time.

The main implication of these successive lines of thought is that, whatever may have been true in the more or less recent past, it has by now become excessively unwise for socialists to settle upon too specific and imperious conceptions of the intrinsically desirable without paying close attention to the practicalities of social and political action. Socialist criticisms of the inheritance of massive economic privilege or of the acquisition or consumption of great wealth without a clear relation to social contribution follow comfortably the grain of modern moral sensibility and belief. What obstructs the political implementation of this sensibility is on the whole a severely practical matter: the unintended consequences of the tentative steps so far taken to implement the criticisms and the effective defensive advantages of those who stand to lose from their implementation.

III.

The third demand which it is reasonable to make of a political theory is that it should tell us, at least broadly, what is to be done to realize in practice as intrinsically desirable a social and political condition as can in fact be realized and sustained in the historical circumstances in which we find ourselves.

It is this third desideratum which is by far the most important aspect of a political theory. It is on balance helpful in politics, as in other branches of human life, for men and women to have a clear and accurate sense of the conditions in which they find themselves. It is instructive and salutary to possess a confident and coherent conception of what in politics deserves to be valued and sustained. But it is indispensable for human beings to understand as well as they can what they should do to maintain the better aspects of the society to which they belong and to improve its worst aspects to the best of their abilities.

IV.

It would be unwise at present to assume that socialism enjoys any very commanding advantages over its practical competitors in any of these three principal aspects of a theory of modern politics. Even the socialist conception of what properties are intrinsically desirable in a society can reasonably be suspected of internal incoherence — to say nothing of the possible exclusion of important economic, social or political goods. Socialist conceptions of the actual character of existing societies, both capitalist and socialist, in all their diversity, can certainly be suspected of undue discretion in the acknowledgement of some of their properties and of a simple failure to recognize others. (Socialism, Marxist or otherwise, is no more a *guarantee* of social understanding than history, or sociology, or neoclassical economics. Nor, for that matter, is it any more than these a conclusive impediment to such understanding.) But both in its grasp of what existing capitalist societies are like and of why they are like this, and in its conception of what aspects of them, other things being equal, are intrinsically regrettable, socialism retains very considerable strength. It is a strength, furthermore, which has been demonstrated very concretely and rather steadily in the historical development of capitalist societies from the early nineteenth century up to at least the early 1970s.[17]

But where socialism at present has become dramatically enfeebled and unpersuasive is precisely in its conception of what it is now prudent and desirable politically to do. Socialist theory in its classical forms, combined with a more or less systematic criticism of the vices of capitalist society and a more or less evocative expression of the presumed superiority of a socialist society, presented a reasonably definite doctrine about how exactly the transition from the bad past to the good future was to be effected. Since the early nineteenth century, socialist doctrine has taken a considerable variety of forms:[18] utopian, revolutionary, gradualist, anarchist, authoritarian, irrationalist. In many cases the rationale of the different forms has rested most directly not on the happy discovery of its own practical efficacy, but on the less encouraging experience of the ineffectiveness or the dismal consequences of one or more of its socialist competitors. If in the course of the last century and a half anyone had succeeded in developing a relatively clear, simple and well-founded conception of how the transition to socialism could in practice be carried through for the better, there is no reason to doubt that this conception would by now have been implemented very widely indeed.

But no one at present knows that the transition to socialism can in fact be carried through for the better, and sustained subsequently once it has been achieved. Except where descriptions of social or political relations are internally contradictory, we cannot accurately be said to *know* anything at all about social or political impossibility. But in assessing social and political impossibility, there is little need for knowledge: a reasonably strong belief will provide all the motivational energy that is likely to be required.

What we certainly do know on this score is that transitions to socialism can be carried through for the worse (the least contestable example would be the case of Kampuchea); and that, at least without foreign intervention, they can

11

then be sustained subsequently as readily as any form of modern state. It would be frivolous to suggest that most aspects of the Soviet Union today represent a marked degeneration from the Russia of the Romanoffs. But what is clear is that the Soviet Union today does represent a very marked degeneration indeed from what any socialist of the early twentieth century was pessimistic enough to imagine as the social and political (perhaps even the economic) consequences of socialism. It is a nice doctrinal issue within socialist dogmatics (the socialist theory of the good applied) whether the Soviet Union should or should not be described as a socialist society. But, as it actually exists, it is at any rate scarcely the sort of society which socialists have had in mind when asserting the superiority of socialism over capitalism.

V.

From the twin facts that no one today knows that the transition to socialism can be carried through for the better and that every western schoolboy or schoolgirl (everyone in a position to take an informed interest in the question) knows that the transition to socialism can on occasion be carried through for the worse, it is easy to see the centrality of the problem of the transition for any serious modern understanding of socialist politics.

The problem can be summed up in two vivid anxieties. First, a revolutionary road to socialism, where this proves to lie open, must pass through immense economic destruction and civil war, and because it must do so, can only be travelled to its end through the construction of massive centralized coercive and organizational power, creating at its outcome a society in which, whatever its economic strengths or weaknesses, tyranny is mitigated only by its pervasive inefficiency. Secondly, a reformist road to socialism, within the framework of capitalist democracy, will always be blocked in the end, either by the formidable obstructive powers which the defenders of private capital in such societies have at their disposal or, if necessary and in the last instance, by a deliberate and brutal suspension of the civil and political rights which their members at present enjoy and which are so grossly and shockingly absent in those socialist states which have emerged from revolution or from territorial conquest by other socialist states.

In the rhetoric of socialist political dispute what is highlighted within these two anxieties is not always what is of principal significance. In the critique of revolutionary politics, for example, reformist socialists are apt to concentrate their fire on the deplorable absence of moral scruple in the pursuit of political goals so common in the Leninist tradition and not on the purely causal insight now offered by history as to what goods (if any) such conduct has the capacity to attain.[19] In the critique of reformist politics, analogously, revolutionary socialists are equally apt to stress the lack of zeal and daring, the sheer pusillanimity, of their gradualist opponents, rather than insisting on the relatively strong inductive reasons for supposing that a political strategy of this character simply can never reach its intended destination. (Or, as Lenin put it to George Lansbury during the latter's visit to the Soviet Union: 'I don't believe you can do it your way. But, if you can, well, do it.')[20]

VI.

Can there then ever be a transition to socialism in practice anywhere (where socialism is understood as the name of at least a coherent and morally defensible core of notions which lie at the centre of a socialist conception of the good)? And if, for any reason, there cannot be such a transition, what exactly does that mean for the political status and prospects of socialist politics?

It is apparent enough that such a possibility (if it were identified and acknowledged) would do more lethal damage to a revolutionary than to a gradualist conception of socialism. The indispensability of revolution, in the understanding of revolutionaries, is not (or at least not mainly) a function of the invigorating qualities of the process of revolution itself, but simply a clear index of the categorical change between one mode of social, economic and political organization and another. The drastic remedy of revolution matches the completeness of the transformation which is required and which can then and only then be carried out. By contrast, gradualist socialists (the revisionist Bernstein, the renegade Kautsky, the European socialist parties following the foundation of the Third International, the British tradition of Parliamentary socialism) have found themselves throughout rather readily persuaded that such transformation, whether or not it is practically out of the question, is in fact unnecessary to realize many of the goals which they wish to reach, and often indeed that it might in practice prove on balance not altogether desirable. What to a confident revolutionary socialist would be nothing but purely external obstruction and frustration, to a more nervous reformist readily becomes a helpful, if initially involuntary, lesson in prudence. (Do not run before you can walk. Do not destroy what you have no idea whatever how to rebuild etc.).

In what follows I argue, along reformist lines, that there is in fact overwhelmingly good reason to take the variety of obstructions which have by now been encountered in the course of attempted transitions to socialism as helpful lessons in prudence: that earlier interpretations of socialism have proved politically feckless to a degree; that no version of revolutionary socialism which deserves the faintest trace of moral or political respect can justify the ignoring of such lessons; and that the attempt to draw these as accurately and to absorb them as deeply as possible is indispensable to the reconstruction of any intellectually serious understanding of socialist politics and a necessary preliminary to adjudicating the respective political merits and limitations of reformist or revolutionary socialism. (Since any form of socialist politics is a human practice, it is certain to have limitations, equally certain to have some point, but wholly uncertain in the first instance to possess any consequential merits.)

VII.

The initial stimulus to the writing of this essay (as is no doubt apparent) was the outcome of the 1983 British General Election, an event of modest local importance but scarcely of much historical significance. In the face of a particularly destructive conservative government and a level of unemployment unknown for nearly half a century, the British electorate divided its favours between a somewhat reduced support for the incumbent government, a somewhat increased support for a recently formed centrist alliance (including a number of former members of the right wing of the Labour Party), and a sharply reduced support for a Labour Party in which the political centre of gravity had shifted considerably to the left. Under the British electoral system the outcome of this pattern of voting was the return of a considerably strengthened conservative government, actively committed to the continuation and intensification of its existing policies of lowering public expenditure, extending the scope of market relations and diminishing the extent and level of public welfare provision.

Many aspects of the causation of this outcome were of narrowly local significance, particularly those bearing directly on the experience of armed conflict and the personality of the Prime Minister. Others, while conspicuous enough (like the attempt to divide the Labour Party or the increased animosity of the major news media to the more explicitly socialist residue of the Labour Party), shed little illumination on the nature of socialist politics. But one aspect of the causation is of some general importance: the relation between explanations of the outcome and assessments of political responsibility for its occurrence.

VIII.

The key consideration here is that the outcome in question was the result of a democratic election: an expression of popular electoral will. Democracy notoriously has (and always has had) many limitations. Populaces, like individuals, can be and quite often are confused, greedy or nervous. At the point at which a legislative election takes place, voters are given only the opportunity to choose between a small number of not necessarily very enticing or reassuring options. It is always open to rejected politicians to fix the blame for their mishaps as firmly as they can on the myopia, vice or folly of the people: 'Once again', as Engels complained in the electoral aftermath

14

of 1867, 'the proletariat has discredited itself terribly.'[21] But although it is always open to rejected politicians to adopt this attitude, it is seldom or never either becoming or intelligent of them to do so. It is unbecoming, because candidates for democratic political leadership must at least affect to compete for the political support and allegiance of voters and party members by appearing, as convincingly as they can, to deserve this. It is unintelligent because the myopia, vice or folly of the people, insofar as these defects can be validly claimed to exist, are either intractably given causal factors which it is the responsibility of candidates for political leadership to take fully into account and to adjust their dispositions towards, or they are potentially modifiable qualities of the perception and judgement of the people which it is even more clearly the responsibility of candidates for political leadership to enlighten as fully as possible. Considered wholly causally and hierarchically, the political dispositions of a demos are simply the materials through which political leaders in a democracy must work if they are to have the opportunity to work at all. To blame the materials, in this perspective, is simply incoherent: a bad workman blames his tools. But in a less cynical and alienated perspective such blame is merely impertinent. Democracy is not a one-way didactic exercise. In a democracy political leaders certainly address the consciousness of the demos; but leaders who are democrats themselves do not merely address the consciousness of the demos or take wary practical account of its content, they also attend to it and try as best they can to respond to it.[22] On a democratic understanding of democracy, therefore, it is a difficult feat, at least for those fortunate enough to find themselves at the head of an established political party, for political leaders to lose an election unless, in the last instance, to lose it is what they deserve.

This is in no sense a sentimental view. Political competition at any point in any real society is not a free and open debate between equals on what exactly is good and true. (It is no easy matter to identify the conditions in which such debates could take place.[23] But what is quite clear is that these conditions could not be satisfied in the national politics of any existing society as these are now organized.) It is perfectly correct to maintain, for example, that in modern capitalist societies the majority of the population are educated extensively and in a rich variety of ways to equate the requirements for capitalist production with the requirements for organized social life. (It is distinctly less correct to assume that there are no ways in which any of them are educated to take a different view; and even further from the truth, of course, to suppose that all of them are deeply convinced of the validity of this educational message in the light of their experience of many other features of their lives.) It is also true that in a modern capitalist society most of the major news media, whether privately or publically owned, most of the time tend to endorse the validity of this educational message and to reinforce its impact as effectively as they can. And it should hardly be a matter for surprise that

15

where the electorate are presented with a choice between a strongly socialist political programme and what is at least intended as a vigorous defence of capitalist interests, those major news media which are privately owned should for the most part align themselves with some vehemence in favour of the latter and against the former.

To seek to transform a capitalist into a socialist society is necessarily to struggle politically against elaborate and powerful resistance. But in countries like England or Scotland in which over the last century and a half only a handful of men or women have been deliberately killed by the state in the course of domestic class conflict,[24] it is absurd to exaggerate the pathos of this struggle. As Marx prophesied, and as capable conservative leaders have consistently rediscovered, to seek to prevent a capitalist society from being transformed more or less steadily and rapidly into a socialist society it is also necessary to struggle politically against elaborate and powerful resistance (though the resistance in this case naturally comes from different quarters). The comparison between the society and economy of Britain in 1900 and in 1970 makes it extremely clear that the expression of domestic class conflict through democratic competition for control over the state has moved the country a considerable distance away from a classically capitalist society and towards a socialist one. (A considerable distance must not be mistaken for the whole way; but it must also not be mistaken for no distance at all.) It was by advocating and in part carrying through just this movement that the British Labour Party at its zenith won the electoral support of almost half the voting population of the country and that it has retained a large, though diminishing, proportion of this allegiance until very recently indeed. It would be absurd to claim that the ideological content of British public education or the extent of capitalist control over the major news media has been dramatically greater over the last three years than it used to be three decades ago. In the days when the Labour Party held a steady grip on the electoral support of a substantial majority of the British industrial working class, this was a grip which it won and retained by its own political insight and exertions. What caused the dramatic collapse in its electoral support in the election of 1983 was a sharp decline in its political credibility, a decline for which only the party itself, along with a selection of its more prominent former members, had any real responsibility at all. To lose the trust of voters in a democratic election is never something for which the leaders of a political party can hope to escape responsibility. To blame the electors for their desertion or, still more, to attribute the responses of the electors to the impairment of their capacities to judge or choose through the malign exertions of others is to repudiate the very modest elements of democracy which the inhabitants of capitalist democracies today enjoy. Given the sinister relation between socialism and tyranny in the present century, there could hardly be a less reassuring response to socialist electoral defeat.

Whatever else may have been true of the British General Election of 1983, one thing which is perfectly clear is that this was an election which the British Labour Party richly deserved to lose.

IX.

To determine exactly why it did deserve to do so is, naturally, more complicated and contentious. Was it, for example, because the decisively socialist programme which it offered to the electorate (heavy public spending to escape from recession; sharp increases in marginal tax rates; a combination of controlled prices with 'free collective bargaining'; withdrawal from the European Common Market; unilateral nuclear disarmament – with some equivocations; state direction of investment; import controls; the creation of a siege economy etc.) was one which large elements of its own leadership regarded with gratuitous and disreputable aversion? Was it because these same presumptively socialist elements (or at least some of them) aroused in many of its former electoral supporters a wholly appropriate fear? Was it because these same aspects of the programme stimulated a more intense and united opposition to the prospect of a Labour victory by the defenders of private capital? Or was it simply, as the terminology of electoral desertion suggests, that the electors themselves, whether as a result of their own debilities of judgement or vagaries of taste, or as a result of subterranean processes of social and cultural change which are eroding the contours and composition of the traditional industrial working class, could no longer identify the traditional political agency of the British working class as a party which was still truly theirs?

Clearly there is some plausibility to each of these explanations; and still more clearly the practical implications of adopting one might well be drastically at odds with those of adopting another. A party which has recently lost part of its leadership by open political desertion and whose residual leadership is in acute conflict over the desirability and prudence of much of its own programme of government is poorly placed to bid for national political power in a country in the throes of a major recession, with inexorably rising unemployment and a deeply and realistically anxious electorate. Proposals in a capitalist society for major movements in a socialist direction will succeed on different occasions in mustering very different levels of popular support; but, other things being equal, they can certainly expect always to encounter a degree of resistance from capitalist interests which is in direct proportion to the scale of the movement threatened. Quite apart from the massive shift in electoral allegiance away from the Labour Party in the election of 1983, social, economic and cultural change in Britain since 1950 has steadily lessened the extent of quasi-automatic (though not in any sense necessarily unthinking) electoral allegiance to the party amongst

17

that large majority of the British adult population that owns its own labour power and has no direct access to the means of production (or indeed of earning a living) except by selling this to whoever is prepared to buy it.

In a study of British politics itself, it would be principally upon these processes of social and cultural change and on the ideological mutations which have accompanied them that it was appropriate to concentrate. But in an assessment of the political theory of socialism more generally they are of much more marginal interest. For, at least in political theory, the important question is whether any version of socialism does in fact offer to the majority of the population of any country an interpretation of the three main theoretical desiderata, with which we began, which is sufficiently clear and commanding to deserve their rational belief and practical allegiance over any length of time. (In the short term, political choice everywhere is quite often a choice between manifest evils.)

Looked at purely causally, British politics is an articulation, within a changing international environment, of the conflicts between domestic social forces; and as such, accordingly, it is to be explained historically. But considered theoretically, the electoral allegiance of the majority of the industrial working class to a very mildly reformist socialist party is not a self-interpreting political good (or bad), but a historical fact, the felicity or infelicity of which remains eminently open to investigation. (In the context of the present essay, it should be clear, socialism is an analytical term indicating aversion to the private ownership of capital, not a theological term ascribing to or withholding from particular political agencies a condition of supposed grace – or disgrace.) Socialist parties differ very widely indeed in the degree to which they aspire, or contrive, to remove the power of private capital to determine the organization of society, as they do in their assessments of the appropriate political format in which to undertake this task. What they have in common is an aversion to economic privileges unrelated to the discharge of current social functions, and a hostility to permitting the shaping and reshaping of society to be determined by the logic of a process of private economic appropriation.

The view that the Labour Party was (and that in some measure it remains) the party of the working class might in the first instance have been an accurate assessment, on the part of the working class, of the political facilities available to it, and might by now have become an equally accurate but somewhat more despondent assessment of those available to it today. But it might also have been in the first instance (and might still remain today) a political myth, the sway of which over the majority of the working class is historically explicable but in no sense rationally justifiable or politically desirable. And by the same token, its undesirability in the past might just as well have been a consequence either of the enfeeblement and nervousness of its commitment to the attempt to establish a genuinely socialist society,[25] or of its ill-considered readiness throughout to make any moves at all in a socialist direction.[26] Given the very low rate of profitability in industrial investment in Britain and the extremely low rate of growth in the gross national product since the Second World War, there is at least some reason to take seriously the common element in these last two judgements. British social democracy, or Parliamentary socialism, has hardly yet fulfilled Macaulay's early-nineteenth-century prophecy that the consequences of universal adult suffrage would be the destruction of civilized society through the use of its capital stock for current consumption.[27] (The present conservative government in Britain might well be thought to have gone further in this direction than any of its Labour predecessors.) But it certainly has underlined the difficulty of combining extensive economic redistribution and some measure of protection against the rigours of the market for the majority of the population with high rates of capital investment and economic growth. Even in the course of a major recession an unequivocally undemocratic socialism is not an enticing offer within a capitalist democracy which is still in operation; but there do nevertheless by now appear to be some fairly persistent internal contradictions within the political project of social democracy.

Some of these contradictions may be purely economic; and it is hard to tell from the case of Great Britain alone how far they are genuinely consequences of the broadly social democratic politics which held sway in the country from the end of the Second World War up to the late 1970s, and how far they are predictable consequences of the working of a particular capitalist economy with a highly distinctive structure and history. Some of the contradictions, however, are more plausibly seen as specifically political in nature. At the level of personal class identification, for example, the British Conservative Party is still characteristically seen, both by those who dislike it and by those who support it, as a natural party of government: a party of those who expect to rule; expect to be obeyed for the most part in doing so; feel no reluctance to assume the responsibilities of doing so and, if necessary, have little hesitation in compelling the obedience of those that prove unready to obey them or disposed to obstruct them in discharging these responsibilities. But the British working class as a whole neither expects to, nor genuinely aspires to, rule. It does not even look to its own political party essentially as an agency of rule, of the systematic exercise of (no doubt, morally disciplined and informed) coercion on behalf of its interests and against those forces which threaten these interests. It does not expect to shape society and is unwilling to undertake the responsibility of attempting to do so. What it expects (and has for some decades in considerable measure received) is protection by the state through legislative intervention at work or through its own defensive organizations, the trade unions, against the more destructive and unpleasant threats of a market society. From the viewpoint of Marx's political hopes this is, of course, a scandal. But since, as André Gorz, for example, has recently pointed out, Marx's political hopes in this respect were never very coherent or well considered,[28] the scandal in this instance lies mainly in the eye of the beholder. Even in an individual a zest to take responsibility for shaping the whole of society indicates at best an impressively Platonic moral austerity and at worst a truly megalomaniac self-regard. We need not, in the first instance at least, be either astounded or disturbed if the majority of the population of a country fails to display any such zest.

X.

A political party is a representative political agency. Even in a state in which every adult member of the population was more or less forcibly incorporated into a single political party, the party would remain in the last instance a representative political agency, since there are no parties (least of all monopolistic ones) which lack a structure of authority, whether this is conceived as principally advisory and inspirational in character or whether it is frankly acknowledged to be explicitly coercive in the last or earlier instances. Because socialist thinkers have set a high value on the transparency of social relations and because they have for the most part retained the classical republican emphasis on the duty of activist civic participation,[29] they have often had severe doubts over the legitimacy of representative political agency. But since effective political agency, in circumstances of the least pragmatic urgency, requires in practice a measure of alienation by most members of a society or association of their opportunity to judge and choose politically,[30] few socialist thinkers engaged in active political struggle have found it attractive to forgo the manifest convenience of political representation. The tension between these two desires has resulted in a systematic disingenuousness or feebleness in socialist thinking on the central questions of practical politics. (In those versions of socialism which centre more or less dogmatically on the allegedly world-historical and emancipatory role of the industrial working class, this disingenuousness has often taken a particularly ludicrous and ugly form in which a real party and an equally real class are equated, with brazen effrontery, by nothing more substantial or material than bare fiat.)

Socialist aversion to political hierarchy and a political division of labour (expressed most clearly and unequivocally, perhaps, in Marx's celebration of the Paris Commune in *The Civil War in France*)[31] is linked profoundly with the socialist conception of the good. It is also intimately connected with the historical experience of resistance to tyranny and oppression. A political division of labour, whether or not it openly acknowledges this consequence, necessarily ensures a measure of real political inequality. The more urgent the practical need for its existence, the more clearly the political inequality in question will prove to be a form of rule. In any historical circumstances, of course, in which human beings were fortunate enough to find themselves without a need for effective political representation, it would be otiose to create a form of political authority and foolish as well as degrading to establish or even voluntarily to tolerate the existence of any form of authority which was genuinely coercive, genuinely a form of rule. But the history of socialism, like the rest of the political history of the human race, lies very far indeed away from such Elysian conditions; and there is every reason to expect it to remain very far away for the imaginable future, in the tense and unstable world of modern nation states with their appalling capacities for destruction. As long as there has to be politics, there will have to be, and will still more certainly continue in fact to be, both political organization and political leadership. The urgency of the need to change the world is not a reliable index of the degree to which it can be changed in practice and it is no index at all of the degree to which it can be trusted to succeed in changing itself. It is, therefore, an extremely important suspicion about socialism that the hypnotic attractions of its conceptions of the social good fatally impair its capacity to speak honestly about practical problems of political organization or to act prudently to resolve them. In the political circumstances directly encountered by historical societies (unlike in Elysium, where political needs no longer obtain) the need for effective and trustworthy political representation is the most urgent of all political needs.

XI.

It is certainly an oversimplification of the problems of socialist politics (and would be so clearly in the case of Great Britain) to see these simply in terms of the political representation of a single class, the industrial working class, by a single party, the party of the proletariat. (In Italy the party of the proletariat, for better or worse, is presumptively the Italian Communist Party, the PCI; but in Britain, if the proletariat has any party at all, that party must indisputably be the Labour Party. The relations between parties and classes at a particular time are matters of historical fact, not of *a priori* dogmatics.) But, although it would be inadequate as a basis for comprehensive political understanding, the relation between a single class and the party which has long most effectively claimed to represent this class will serve well enough as a setting in which to consider the nature of socialist political representation.

The principal qualities required in an individual political representative or in a representative political agency are those of trustworthiness and efficacy. The more independent the agency in question, the greater its capacity to act effectively in the face of contingencies. In war, in the participatory democracy of ancient Athens as in the Britain of 1940, the urgency of the need for efficacy was recognized by according to particular political authorities an extremely high degree of freedom of action. By the same token, the less

21

independent the agency in question, the less the need to trust it. Participatory democracy as a political form minimizes the need for political trust; but it also minimizes the capacity to act briskly in the face of contingency. The command structure of a system of ballistic missiles armed with nuclear warheads has a stunning capacity to respond effectively to one sort of contingency; but it carries the need for trust appallingly much further than human beings have ever had occasion to extend this before, and further perhaps than it could ever rationally stretch.

In the condensed and erratic violence of most revolutions, and in the herculean tasks of social and economic reconstruction set by the devastation which results from most revolutions, the political need for efficacy is especially obvious. (It is important to be clear that it is the scale of the tasks to be undertaken from which the need arises, and that this scale is in no sense an artefact of the more or less absurd or discreditable political presumptuousness of those who have the nerve to undertake these tasks.) Such conditions are as far as possible from Elysium. Not merely was the Paris Commune, as Marx himself observed, only the rising of a single city and without any real potential to become anything more,[32] it was also an unsuccessful rising. Ineffective revolutionaries simply face defeat; and if revolutionary politics can be justified at all – if it amounts to anything more than a sentimental or cynical adventurism – it can be justified only by its success. This is, notoriously, the central message of the politics of Leninism, a political tradition which has shaped much of the history of the twentieth century and which has deformed to some degree the political character of every supposedly representative political agency which it has touched, both from within and from without, by inspiration or defensive reaction. It would be hard to exaggerate the menace of its combination of social transparency as proclaimed destination with the radical commitment to efficacy at the expense of any other competing value in the Long March towards it.

Leninism has an extremely distinctive and complicated history of its own; and the casuistry of its integrity or corruption, its correct or erroneous application, remains bewilderingly intricate. But the key paradox of revolutionary politics, which is wholly distinct from the history of supposedly Leninist political practice, can be stated very simply. It is that any realistic conception of revolutionary practice must lay great emphasis upon efficacy (and acknowledge accordingly the alienation of political choice, will and judgement which this demands); and yet the degree of trust in the political discernment and benignity of the representative political agency of revolution which this recognition entails is in practice little less extreme than the degree of trust which the supposed controllers of the power of nuclear destruction in fact require of us. Anyone who finds it hard to reconcile themselves calmly to the degree of political alienation of our executive power of the law of nature, the extent of sovereign prerogative,[33] constituted by nuclear weapons systems ought to think very carefully indeed about the prudential justification of deliberately revolutionary politics. (The most eirenic and sober of real political agencies may well have thrust upon them political conflicts of extreme violence. But revolutionaries deliberately court such conflicts.) By the same token, those who are relatively untroubled by entrusting to political leaders (for whom in other respects they may have extremely little regard) the practical power to end human life on earth need not be astonished at the readiness of societies which can no longer go on in the old way to entrust the most draconic levels of coercive authority to those who volunteer more or less convincingly to guide them to a new and better way.

XII.

Just as modern states in general and capitalist democracies in particular claim to speak on behalf of all their citizens and to act in defence of the interests of them all, so a proletarian party claims to speak and act on behalf of all the members of the (not perhaps sociologically very clearly demarcated) working class. There is, of course, in reality a large measure of ideological fiction in any such claims. The government of the United Kingdom at present manifestly does not represent the beliefs or sentiments of a large section of the Catholic population of Northern Ireland. The government of Afghanistan at present mahifestly does not represent the beliefs or sentiments of a large proportion of its own rural population. In any country, like France or Italy, in which there exists more than one substantial socialist party claiming to represent the beliefs and interests of the working class, the pretension to monopolistic representation is evidently a little absurd. But it is possible and helpful to consider the nature of the claim without presuming its validity in any particular instance (or perhaps even its potential validity in any actual instance at all).

There are at least three important components in political representation: the social identities of individual citizens, social groupings or social classes and the more or less authoritative institutions which aspire to or pretend to express these identities; the practical content of the interests of individual citizens, groups or social classes and the more or less authoritative institutions which seek to ascertain what the content of these interests at a particular time actually amounts to; and the, again more or less authoritative, institutions which seek to serve and defend the content of these interests in practical political struggle. It is apparent enough that these components are closely connected with one another. No political party of the working class could hope to defend what it took to be the current interests of that class at all effectively unless the working class paid the party in question the compliment of identifying with it. No political party of the working class could even attempt to defend the interests of the latter without presuming that it had broadly succeeded in ascertaining the current content of the interests of the class. And so on.

But although these components are clearly interconnected, their relationships with one another in real historical situations are often uncomfortable and inharmonious. The political identification of an individual or a class with a political party depends upon the subjective sense of identity of the agent or class in question. It is an expressive and not an instrumental relationship. Democratic politics is largely an exercise in competing to secure, retain or subvert such identifications. The psychic mechanism of identification is indisputably subjective, however large a part in the competition to secure it may be played by allegations about the content of individual or class interests. In the politics of capitalist democracies (as indeed in all political processes which involve a struggle to capture or hold the allegiance of large proportions of an adult population), the attempt to reinforce or overthrow such identifications lies at the centre of the struggle between class interests. Not merely does the moulding and remoulding of men's and women's sense of their politically relevant social identities have the most dramatic political consequences; it is also in fact true today, both in capitalist democracies and in *soi-disant* socialist states, that the actual character of their sense of politically relevant social identity for the vast majority of the population is in fact constantly being modified and remoulded by a process of overt or subterranean political struggle. In *soi-disant* socialist states, at least at some points, the principal agents of such modification and remoulding have been ruling and monopolistic political parties. But in relatively modern capitalist states, with the exception of a small number of ghetto political parties (the SPD in Wilhelmine Germany, the French and Italian Communist Parties over the last few decades), political parties have not on the whole played a very prominent role in the shaping of social identities:[34] certainly a far less prominent role than television, radio, newspapers, advertising and the mass consumption of material goods. No populace presented with the choice between having its social identities reshaped gently by the mass consumption of material goods or a little more bracingly by a ruling and monopolistic political party has so far opted firmly for the latter alternative.

It is not hard to see why.

XIII.

Every human being occupies a multiplicity of social roles, stretching all the way from inhabitant of the planet to maiden aunt or obese libertine. The relative salience of these roles shifts steadily under ecological pressure from the outside and by interpretation and active exploration or denial from

24

within. An individual's sense of his social and personal identity, of who and what he is, is a fugitive and shadowy reality; but for individuals at any given time it is the most intense, the truest and the most significant reality there is. In political terms this intense subjectivity of human identity is both a continuing affront and a recurrent practical impediment to professional politicians. The political imagination is busy, manipulative and didactic. It is apt to regard the failure of particular human beings to respond to its importunities as both injurious and insulting. (It is so, in fact, in large measure independently of political taste – whether it regards the political task, with Professor Oakeshott,[35] as the maintenance and repair of existing practical contrivances, or whether it sees this task as the creation of transcendently superior arrangements.) The thoughts that human social and political identities are inherently plastic, but that at any particular time they simply are as they are experienced, are uncomfortable thoughts to combine. No sensible and decent person could applaud the fact that all identities (or perhaps even most) are exactly as they happen to be. But it is the mark of a democrat at least to acknowledge fully, and in the first instance indeed to *accept* that they are as they are. The decision to take an active part in political dispute always involves, at least tacitly, a claim to know better than some: those, for example, whose judgement will otherwise determine what is done. (No human being could be so bereft of imagination and the capacity for enjoyment as to lack other rewarding or useful ways of spending their time.) In this sense any decision to take an active part in politics is inherently presumptuous. But the inherent presumption is a motivational precondition for rational political action; it is not in any sense a title to power. With the inherent presumption there comes a right, and perhaps even a duty, to seek to persuade, but there emphatically does not come the least claim to command.

There are no human beings whose sense of social identity is fully and exclusively given for themselves by their membership of the working (or any other) class. Any real working class is made up of the holders of a bewildering range of work occupations, each with its own distinctive features and relations to other work (and leisure) occupations, each set within a particular locality and community with its own history of shared or dissonant experiences. Kinship, education, travel, political activities and the cultural pressures of the media modify the visions of the world, even of the denizens of the most closed of working-class occupational communities.[36] (In advanced industrial societies, because of the rapidity of technological change, there are in fact progressively fewer such closed communities, with restricted migration in and out and strong and deeply shared historical traditions of their own.) As the character of production changes, through technical innovation and international competition, the size and shape of the industrial working class also alters; and in Britain, for example, there is every reason, whether on pessimistic or on optimistic expectations of the prospective future of the economy, to anticipate a further large fall in the size of the industrial working class over the next two or three decades.

The portrayal of the working class and its destiny set out in the political writings of the young Marx incorporates almost none of these features. The imminent destiny of this class in Marx's view was a rapid and drastic simplification in its sense of subjective social identity under the merciless pressures of capitalist competition. The process of psychic erasure would not merely free the class from other competing and essentially delusive allegiances; it would also necessarily educate the class brutally but thoroughly on the content of its interests. On these assumptions, the party of the proletariat would not be (and still more certainly could not remain for any length of time) an alien representative agency instructing the latter on the content of its interests and competing more or less successfully to wean it from its inherited illusions. The history of the labour movement in Europe and elsewhere since 1848, and the history of political agency in the Marxist tradition more particularly, does not merely show, as no Marxist would be likely to deny, that the historical relations between the working class and politics have been enormously more intricate than his initial projection suggested. (It is clear in fact that Marx himself was perfectly well aware that this was bound to be the case.)[37] The same history also shows that any such conception of a natural right to monopolistic representation by a single organized political party of a class supposedly homogeneous in interest and self-consciously aware of so being was bound to prove a pernicious myth.

Today at least, there is plainly no reason whatever for presuming that in any country the appropriate form for the political representation of even the industrial working class is a single political party with a determinate set of beliefs, values and practices. Nor indeed is there any reason to see the industrial working class either domestically or internationally as possessing either a clear inclination or a privileged capacity to shape the society of the future.[38] Nor is there any reason to believe that the majority of the world's population, even in the absence of nuclear war, will necessarily (or even could possibly) come to be members of an industrial working class. For socialism to claim a clear and legitimate title to political power, therefore, it must be able to show that it deserves power. Even for it to claim the rational allegiance of an industrial working class, it must be able to present itself in the guise of a representative political agency which the class itself can reasonably expect to prove trustworthy and effective.

From the point of view of the leaders of a political party, the identification of a class (or indeed of any large group of persons) with their party is principally a political resource. No political party can hope to play an important political role for any length of time unless the guise in which it succeeds in presenting itself evokes some real resonance in the sense of their own social identity actually held by large numbers of human beings. In the practice of politics it is usual, except in the case of deliberately stigmatized social groups, to portray such identification, where rivals succeed in eliciting it, as essentially deceptive, but to construe it in the case of one's own political following as an accurate mirroring of social and political realities. Analytically, however, such distinctions are impossible to defend. The sense of social identity is plastic and ideological. Much of it is certainly compounded of at least partially false beliefs (to say nothing of more or less deplorable sentiments). Some of the false beliefs (aspects of interwar German anti-semitism, of militant Zionism in Israel or Protestant and Catholic bigotry in Belfast today) have appalling consequences. But at any particular time human beings simply have the sense of social identity which they happen to have. That, in large measure, is what makes them who they are. Precisely because it is both irretrievably causally plastic and yet always existentially real, because it cannot in principle be constituted out of nothing but true beliefs, there is no coherent standard against which men's or women's sense of their social identity can be measured: no external criterion in favour of which its scruffy contours and ignoble self-deceptions can be thankfully or commandingly set aside.

Human beings simply are the way they are.

Accordingly, in rejecting the claims of a particular party to be its rightful representative, a class or group of persons is certainly capable of folly; and in espousing a particular party as its own, a class or group can and sometimes does display vice as well as folly. But no party can be *entitled* to represent any class or group which does not see it as, or feel it to be, its own. Political leaders seek to mould the sense of social identity of those whom they aspire to lead, persuading them as best they can to modify this identity in ways which they take to be desirable or advantageous. The securing and retention of the identification of a following is a large part of their task. Because identification involves feelings as well as beliefs, because it is more an expressive than an instrumental relationship, it is by far the most important mode in which political trust is conferred or withheld. Without it, any rational basis for representative political agency would scarcely be conceivable. Since politics is causally so complex and the relations of interest within it are so ambiguous, and since the accurate calculation of the consequences of political action is, except in the most trivial of cases, virtually impossible, no one in conditions of real political action could have good reason to trust anyone else to act on their behalf. In purely instrumental politics, for example, genuine loyalty (as opposed to the instrumental strategy so named by Hirschman)[39] would not be a virtue, but an index of psychic or cognitive debility.

Trust is the most indispensable of political relations. Its distinctive virtues — loyalty, integrity, honesty in the last instance — remain, despite Machiavelli, the most emotive and troubling of political virtues — even though, as

27

Machiavelli also insisted so cogently, in politics no set of such virtues can be a substitute for efficacy.[40] The securing and retention of political trust is at best a makeshift business, the attempt to play upon the sense of social identity of large numbers of human beings by a more or less crude charade of concern, dedication and resolution. In this perspective, political representation readily appears to the fastidious both ugly and incoherent: a matter of deliberately peddling, or involuntarily succumbing to, noble or ignoble lies. But this judgement takes its force from the tacit implication that there exists a real alternative: the Platonic Republic, the party which uniquely recognizes and discharges the destiny of a world-historical class. All such claims rest ultimately on the presumption that there is a genuinely external criterion for social identity (the soul in the eye of God, the Forms, the class in the process of History) in favour of which our actual sense of social identity can and should be set aside. Virtually everyone's sense of social identity, no doubt, could benefit from cognitive editing or supplementation. But because this sense of social identity is always constituted by the actual subjectivity of real historical agents or classes, there can be no external surrogate for it, no authentic alternative to it. Psychically considered, trust is a relationship between subjectivities. It is the political form in which human beings are compelled to recognize in practice − through its presence or its absence − what for them is always the most fundamental aspect of their condition. The need for trust and the possibility of trust, with its ineradicable hazards and equivocations, is the key to men's and women's capacity to live politically with one another. Its strengths and limitations are the strengths and limits of that capacity.[41] Both the promise of an external alternative to the sense of social identity and the offer of a political future in which trust will no longer be necessary involve the denial of fundamental aspects of the human condition, aspects which every human being in their own life necessarily knows to obtain. Neither promise, accordingly, can ever be made by anyone wholly in good faith. But this inescapable degree of insincerity, notoriously, need do little to diminish the vehemence with which the promise itself is offered or the alacrity with which men and women may come to put their trust all too practically in its prospective benefits, at least for a time.

XIV.

The psychic identification of party with class and class with party is, to be sure, only one aspect of a party's capacity to serve as the representative political agency of a class. In a constitutional democracy no party can do much to represent the interests of any class unless quite large numbers of people can identify with its presumed intentions: so the eliciting of some measure of identification is a necessary condition for a political party to represent any interests at all. A party in government might clearly in practice succeed quite effectively in representing the interests of a particular class, most of whose members are quite unable to identify with it. The British Conservative Party, for example, has long claimed to be not merely concerned to represent but also to be highly effective at representing the interests of the British working class. It is not, on the whole, plausible that this has ever been the party's most pressing preoccupation; but, at least consequentially, it is not obvious that its effectiveness at doing so has proved notably inferior to, for example, the services of the Communist Party of the Soviet Union to the Russian working class. (To assess the comparative authenticity and commitment of these two agencies to this representative assignment would be an intriguing but strenuous exercise in political judgement, and it is a mark of the bathetic intellectual vitality of professional political science that at present it could offer so little effective intellectual assistance in making the assessment.) Even the most complete identification between a class and a party, however, falls some way short of being a sufficient condition for effective representative agency by the latter. In considering the party's representative prowess, it is always necessary also to consider its capacity both to ascertain clearly and accurately where the interests of its constituency in fact lie and to defend these interests successfully in political struggle wherever this proves to be required.

In this last undertaking, the trust of a class is an unambiguous asset: the more enduring and the more compulsive the greater the asset. The loyalty of class to party is not merely a structure of human meaning of major importance in the lives of particular human beings, it is also a formidable political resource. In particular, on the often disadvantageous terrain of political conflict, it makes it possible for political leaders to pursue long-term and carefully considered policies, rather than reacting nervously to a flurry of immediate contingencies. It strengthens their nerves and capacities for resistance and widens their field of manoeuvre. It also makes it possible for them to secure considerable short-term sacrifices from their followers, to induce a voluntary acceptance of the delayed gratification on which almost all substantial human progress has always depended. (All this perhaps suggests that loyalty might indeed be a good instrumental strategy in Hirschman's terms. But it would not, of course, be an actual political possibility in a social setting where most of the human agents did in fact think in Hirschman's terms.)

In political competition, the trusted party of a trusting class will always prove a formidable political opponent and, at least in a constitutional democracy, a party trusted by no class at all will make little durable political impact. But since trust in this sense is simply a matter of psychic identification and since there is no external standard by which to appraise psychic identification (since the force of psychic identification is not subject to external appraisal), its actual distribution at any particular time can only be taken as a given. By consequential standards, it may well be, and perhaps often is, unwise of a particular class to trust a particular party; and allegations about the wisdom or unwisdom of so doing always figure prominently in the practical struggle to mould political identification. But at any given point in time, the decisive fact for a particular group or class must always be that it does or does not trust each particular contender to represent its interests. The rational basis for political identification is the assessment of the capacities of a would-be representative agency to ascertain accurately the content of the interests of a given group or class or alliance of classes and to defend these effectively in the course of political struggle.

One of the classic dilemmas of socialist theory is posed by the evident potential contradiction between the conditions which are propitious for these last two capacities. Because of the enormous importance of effective coordination in a complex struggle, the requirements of political combat can readily be judged to dictate a clear hierarchy of authority with a massive concentration of power at its summit. The particular conditions of struggle against the Tsarist autocracy, in Lenin's famous *What is to be Done?*, were therefore judged to require a combination of centralization of authority and clandestinity which has shown a remarkable longevity.[42] How far political efficacy did in fact preclude a more democratic structure of party authority was keenly disputed by Russian socialists at the time.[43] It is important also that in the same work Lenin should have expressed a particularly sharp contempt for the capacities of the Russian proletariat to ascertain for itself the content of its own interests. To the contender to establish enduring socialist rule, 'trade-union consciousness' is a disappointing form for the class consciousness of the proletariat to assume. But there seems little doubt by now that it is an overwhelmingly more frequent form for this consciousness to assume in capitalist societies at most stages of their history than a clear desire or hope on the part of the class as a whole to take and exercise state power – let alone a confident expectation that it possesses the capacity to do so.[44] But whether or not 'trade-union consciousness' does embody an accurate appraisal of the interests of the industrial working class, and whether or not at any point in his life the judgements of Lenin himself did embody a more accurate appraisal of these interests are far from being self-evident. To answer such questions requires an extremely complicated consequential and counterfactual assessment; and although it is possible to describe the issues with reasonable clarity, and although most politically interested persons are apt to be exceedingly confident in their verdicts, it cannot really be said at present that anyone has yet advanced a very convincing account of how such assessments should be carried out.

It is indeed not even clear that the model of pyramidal authority does give a particularly good account of the requirements for effective combat. Here the powerful tradition of analysis of military organization is clearly relevant.

Certainly there are no very effective modern armies in which the commands of the Commander-in-Chief do not enjoy final military authority. But there are also very wide variations in the degree of initiative left open to, and in fact assumed by, subordinate commanders down to the smallest military units; and it seems clear that the most effective modern armies require and display a high degree of independent initiative diffused throughout their ranks. They need to do so precisely because of the problems of coordinating accurately the activities of large numbers of human beings in conditions about which no single person can be fully informed and which change rapidly and unexpectedly. In politics, as in war, as Clausewitz insisted,[45] the crucial fact is that things never go according to plan. (It has proved to be an extremely important limitation of socialist economic planning that the amount of information required for rational choice at the centre of an economy can never in practice be secured there, and that it is virtually impossible in consequence, within the confines of a centralized command economy, to respond efficiently to the – virtually uninterrupted – experience of deviations from initial expectations. The massive advantages of the market mechanism from this point of view are the degree to which it economizes on information and the relative rapidity with which it responds to changes in expectation.)[46] To work effectively, it is indispensable for human organizations to be well adapted to whatever degree of partial ignorance of the conditions in which they have to operate is ineliminable. This is perhaps the most important single practical implication of the profound untransparency of human social relations. It is one which Marx himself,[47] and nineteenth-century socialist thinkers in general, utterly failed to confront.

The suspicion that the Leninist party is not in fact organizationally well designed to represent the interests of the proletariat is fairly widespread, even inside Leninist parties (particularly where these do not hold governmental power), though it naturally has to be voiced more discreetly within the latter. Too much of the behaviour of these parties is a product of imperative coordination and not enough of unsanctioned rational discussion amongst what are genuinely recognized to be political equals. But the most important doubt about Leninist parties arises not over their efficacy as combat organizations – the task for which they are exclusively and a trifle simple-mindedly designed – but over the degree to which they can rationally be trusted to succeed in ascertaining and seeking to promote the interests of the proletariat. (On a disabused and cynical account, it has by now become in many instances simply an index of sentimentality to suppose that Leninist parties, particularly in government, retain the faintest interest in ascertaining the interests of the class which they claim to represent. Proletarian representation, accordingly, is merely an ideological fig-leaf behind which to hide a morbid lust for power as such. But this mode of cynicism is at root excessively moralistic since it neglects, in very understandable revulsion, the

31

fact that success in serving the interests of the proletariat, other things being equal, would be an overwhelming asset for the existing leadership of the party in their, sometimes taxing, struggle to retain power.)

XV.

Here it may be helpful to contrast a liberal (or democratic) model of a socialist party with an authoritarian (or Leninist) model of such a party. The liberal model places its main emphasis on the difficulty in principle for a dominant authority to acquire accurate information about the interests of those whom it controls and on the insufficient force of the incentives for such an authority to seek this information consistently and urgently, or to act upon it at all punctiliously. It combines, that is to say, two of the principal liberal preoccupations: the supposedly superior capacity of individuals to ascertain their own interests, and the desirability of economizing on trust in the design of human political institutions (not because the latter can ever be wholly dispensed with, but because it is inherently hazardous). Since a successful political party will exercise rule, it is only prudent to consider the authority structure of a political party itself as a fully political institution: as incipiently itself a form of rule.

Each of these liberal themes deserves some attention. The first is, notoriously, more than a little problematic. Do human beings really know what they want? As to what I want myself, I am no doubt the world's leading authority; but the incessant pressures of regret certainly establish that even I am an eminently fallible authority. The egalitarian liberal insistence equivocates more or less steadily between the trivial truism that every person prefers their own preferences and the striking falsehood that all human beings always know best what is in their interest. Because of the large cognitive element in the appraisal of interest that is furnished, at the very least, by its dependence on future contingencies, it is only too clear that human beings can be comprehensively mistaken over what is to their advantage, while they can at worst be selectively inattentive to what it is that they do at a particular moment specifically happen to desire. The immediacy and authority of present desire is more than offset, for purposes of political alignment and action, by its rapid evanescence. The view that every person is best placed to assess their own interests is therefore better seen as a somewhat bleary prudential reminder of the hazards of permanently alienating such assessment to any other person or institution than as a defensible axiom in a theory of the human good. In this light, accordingly, the two liberal themes coalesce into one: a prudential emphasis on the perils of political power.

One way of conceiving a political party is to see it as an organization specifically designed to inquire into and form well-founded beliefs about the content of the interests of its members (and whoever else they hold dear). In this sense a party aspires to be a learning device for its members – and one which may well modify the attitudes and sentiments as well as the causal beliefs of the latter. The grounds for preferring a liberal democratic model for a party rest largely, though not exclusively, on this role. An organization in which all the members are officially acknowledged to enjoy an equal right of political perception and judgement and are entitled, at least in the first instance, to an equal share in political power is ill-placed to ignore the active expression of dissenting views by large numbers of its members. There can be, of course – indeed often are – large and systematic differences between the beliefs and attitudes of the members of a political party and the beliefs and attitudes of the groups or classes for which that party aspires to speak. There is nothing necessarily untoward about the existence of such gaps. It is perfectly legitimate for the members of the party, at least when this is not exercising governmental power (an opportunity which raises other issues), to interpret the existence of such a gap simply as a challenge to their powers of persuasion. What is not legitimate, however, on the liberal democratic understanding, is to presume to speak for the dissenting groups or classes simply on the strength of the cognitive or moral self-assurance of the party's members, or of their experience of the solidarity of the group or class in earlier years.

The crux of the disagreement between partisans of liberal democratic or authoritarian models for the organization of a socialist party comes over the assessment of the capacity of the majority of human beings to see, feel and judge for themselves. Those who distrust the cognitive powers and emotional sensibilities of the majority more than they fear the perils of the abuse of power will probably opt for the latter model, particularly if they contrive to imagine themselves as exercising the power in question. The hazards of this wager are by now reasonably apparent. To insist on the need for a crisp and decisive hierarchical authority in political struggle probably involves some measure of misjudgement of the requirements for effective combat, but is considerably more cogent than a denial that there is any need for authority at all in the coordination of political conflict on a large scale. To insist, however, on the need for an authoritative determination of the content of the interests of the majority by a small minority – and to do so in practice by largely suppressing the opportunities for the majority to reflect systematically and without harassment in public on the content of its own interests – is to confer a quite arbitrary measure of trust on a group of persons who are every bit as fallible as those over whom their authority is to be exerted. Except in the face of gross oppression, this measure of trust is one which no human organization could ever defensibly claim. And if it is offensively presumptuous in a party competing freely for the support of citizens, it is a criminal abuse in a party which has secured control over the governmental machinery of a modern state. A socialist party may propose to its constituency the boldest of interpretations of the content of their interests. It may reasonably aspire to win their unthinking loyalty and to secure their fervent belief in its capacities to identify these interests accurately and to serve them effectively. What it cannot in honour do is explicitly to impose its own interpretation of the content of these interests against the judgement of the constituency itself and, if necessary, over their more or less active resistance.

Neither kings nor socialist parties enjoy a divine right to rule.[48]

XVI.

The key question for the political theory of socialism, accordingly, is always that of how far any single interpretation of the appropriate content of socialist politics at a particular time does offer sufficient basis for a right to rule. It is, indeed, a mark of the political seriousness of socialism that it acknowledges the need for rule in the relevant future, however democratically it hopes that such rule may come to be exercised. It is, that is to say, democratic in the last instance, as opposed to anarchist. Optimistic democrats may hope that in a happier future very little, if any, rule will prove to be required, though only very silly democrats will actually expect this future to arrive. What distinguishes an optimistic democrat from even the most pessimistic of anarchists is the recognition that there are many human goods on behalf of which men and women have every right to exert, and may well often face the need to exert, such organized coercive force as they can muster. Anarchists are sometimes gleefully destructive in the face of existing coercive power.[49] But they cannot bring themselves to recognize simultaneously both the range of practical threats which real human beings in real social settings pose to one another and the intricate and always partially unsuccessful requirements for mustering organized coercive force in order to avert these threats.

To claim such a right to rule with justification, a socialist party would need ideally to possess an understanding of the society as it is which showed socialist policies to be a necessary remedy for, or at least a beneficial alleviation of, some of its major existing demerits and to threaten none of its existing merits. Its policies, that is to say, must combine an accurate assessment of the causal properties of the existing society, a coherent and well-judged conception of a superior set of social arrangements, and both a realistic appreciation of and a practical respect for the degree to which the existing society could in practice be transformed into this superior set of arrangements. A party which stood in this relation to the society to which it belonged would objectively possess a programme which, other things being equal, would equip and entitle it to rule.

Other things, however, might prove to be unequal in a variety of different ways. For one thing, the possession of such an ideal degree of social and political understanding would scarcely be a necessary condition under most circumstances for possessing qualifications to rule superior to those of any other effective contender. At least in terms of the cognitive adequacy of their political programmes, the party best equipped to rule will simply be the party whose political programme is superior in cognitive adequacy to those advanced by its competitors. For another thing, the party fortunate enough to possess this superior social and political understanding might also be so unfortunate as to lack the trust or identification of any substantial portion of the citizenry. Furthermore, since even the most discerning and trustworthy of political parties must at some point start from scratch in mustering their followings, the absence of such identification is no index of demerit. But on the liberal democratic, unlike the authoritarian, interpretation of socialist politics, it unquestionably does imply the absence of a current right to rule.

Even a party with an impeccable programme and a substantial and enthusiastic following may not prove especially effective at ruling, or even particularly successful in securing the opportunity to rule. Besides a practical skill at political administration (and the understanding of social dynamics, which is a precondition for this in the modern world) and a moral sensitivity to human goods, a political party requires a quite distinct competitive skill: the capacity to win and hold the support of men and women and to secure and retain the practical opportunity to defend their interests in the violent and exacting arena of political conflict. Parties can possess this skill, and display it with some *éclat*, despite the most grotesque cognitive deformations in their political programmes. In a grim way, the Bolshevik Party between 1917 and 1944 arguably did so; and from the point of view of more intrepid socialists (or the followers of Mrs Thatcher) the British Labour Party has also done so for much of the past four decades. An ideal political party, accordingly, would need to display great depth of social understanding and executive skill in realizing its social aspirations, with equal resolution in political combat and equal skill in defeating its adversaries in this combat. In practice, of course, parties display these merits in very different proportions and the virtues which they require in leaders and members are often distressingly at odds with each other: openness, decency and scruple against daring, energy and will – a sad pessimism of the will against a ludicrous optimism of what passes for the intelligence etc.

ʊʊ

Democratic socialism as a political practice

XVII.

Socialist politics, I have argued, like any other form of politics, is intricate and ambivalent. It is an attempt to modify the real social world in desirable directions, not a prophetic venture in summoning up Elysium. Under socialism, in any of its vast variety of possible forms, men and women will be a bit different from how they are under capitalism, in its no less multifarious variety: just as we are a bit different from the cast of the *Iliad* or the Icelandic Sagas, or from the Trobriand islanders or the Nuer of half a century ago. What they will certainly not be, as Trotsky vapidly suggested, is utterly and splendidly different.[50] Nor will socialist societies, insofar as these are actually created, and even if they do succeed in representing a major improvement on existing schemes of social organization, prove to consist of nothing but humanly desirable states of affairs.

One major impediment to thinking about socialism is the practice of using the term to refer not to sets of specifiable human institutions, actual or potential, but to purely imaginary and stipulatively ideal conditions. About ideal socialism of this character there is no possibility of rational learning, since the discouraging lessons of historical experience are inevitably held to have no bearing upon it. Between any forms of socialism that actually exist and any form of socialism genuinely deserving of the title there falls an impermeable curtain of darkness. As it stands, this dogmatic hiatus between the ideal and the experience commits the devotee of true socialism merely to a resolute imprudence. But by now, mercifully, there seems some reason to believe that it also frequently weakens his or her political appeal.

It is certainly appropriate that it should exert this effect. Political understanding and judgement is difficult enough in principle without conscientiously turning one's back on the major source of relevant insight which is available to guide it. The suspicion that socialists do not really know what they are doing is an extremely damaging suspicion in most competitive political conditions. It can be dissipated, where it can be dissipated at all, only by acknowledging the difficulties and inconveniences which have turned out to accompany the variety of socialist organizational forms and by describing what precise measures the socialist grouping in question proposes to take to meet and overcome these difficulties. One important example of this point is the political lessons offered by the history of the Soviet Union. From a conservative viewpoint it may be sufficient to conclude from this experience that revolution is appallingly costly and that the creation of a tyrannical socialist government which abrogates civil liberties and the rule of law is likely to prove an extremely durable political catastrophe. None of these, of course, are lessons which a socialist need (or should) deny – though many socialists will certainly do their best or worst to do so. But they are decidedly not the only lessons which a socialist needs to draw from this experience. The Soviet Union has unquestionably given grounds to the politically attentive for anxiety about the consequences of the revolutionary road to socialism: more grounds perhaps, thus far, than Mozambique or Nicaragua (early days yet), but dramatically fewer grounds than Kampuchea (where the early days alone were more than enough). But it is not just as an awful warning that Soviet history matters. 'It is impossible for anyone seriously concerned with the future of socialism to ignore the political and social aspects of Soviet reality, and their links with the economic system.'[51] Whatever else socialism may imply and bring about, it does imply at least a mode of organizing some substantial part of the production of a society. The main thrust away from capitalism, at least in socialist theory, comes from the anarchic character of capitalist production. The main pull towards socialism, again within socialist theory, comes from the comparatively rational and ordered character of socialist production and the consequently evident superiority of the latter. Such a comparison was simple and reassuring at a time, like the year 1848, when the anarchy of capitalist production was all too palpable and the orderliness of socialist production was only an attractive idea. But today, where many advanced capitalist countries include elements of socialist production and where there exist whole vast societies in which the great bulk of the means of production has at some time been or even still remains in fully public ownership, the comparison is considerably less simple. It is also in a substantial number of respects far less reassuring.

XVIII.

The centre of socialist political theory – and by far its most robust, enduring and cogent component – has been its understanding of the intrinsic defects of a capitalist mode of production. In Marx's own case this understanding was balanced by a fairly clear sense of the intrinsic merits of capitalism as a mode of production, particularly in comparison with its historical predecessors. On the whole modern socialists, except at times in the western reformist tradition from Eduard Bernstein to Antony Crosland, have not retained a very sharp sense of these merits. The principal theoretical difficulty faced by socialist thinkers since 1917 has been to see just how to balance the intrinsic defects of a capitalist mode of production against the observed (and perhaps equally intrinsic) defects of a socialist mode of production. By the 1980s, at least in relatively advanced capitalist countries, this has ceased to be a purely theoretical difficulty. The extension of public ownership of the means of production in these societies has clearly failed to improve either the productivity of the industries in question or the quality of work experience within them; and in a weak economy like that of Great Britain it has also placed upon the state a progressively more unmanageable fiscal burden. The tax levels which accompanied the extensive redistribution of income and which were required to sustain the relatively high level of minimum welfare that had come to be publicly provided have begun not merely to have alleged disincentive effects on the economic energies of the rich or the leading managerial cadres of large corporative enterprises, but very palpable – and loudly resented – disincentive effects on the labour of the poorer sections of the employed working class, and they have produced a corresponding shift in the proportion of economic exchanges which take place outside the purlieus of the legal economy. Taken individually, these unintended consequences of the extension of socialist production or economic redistribution might well have had no significant effect upon popular enthusiasm for socialism (though it is hard to see how, on their own, they could have increased it). But taken together, they certainly make it unsurprising that a marked shift to the left in the political programmes and attitudes of the Labour Party should have elicited a marked shift to the right in the political allegiance of the British electorate.

Utopian socialism is a form of socialist politics which rests its confidence in the political merits of socialism on the intrinsic charms of its conception of a good society and which trusts that these merits will in due course enforce themselves, by example, upon the refractory political consciousness of the majority. It may be contrasted, at least in the first instance, with forms of socialism which see the latter's political merits and prospects as linked intimately to a clear conception of the demerits of an existing mode of society and to a more or less vivid and definite sense of these demerits experienced by a majority of its inhabitants. In this respect British socialism over the last decade has moved steadily towards the utopian, not because the real grounds for popular discontent in the country have diminished – they have, on the contrary, increased sharply – but because the British socialist account of the causes of and the appropriate remedies for these discontents has drifted markedly further away from that more or less consciously held by the majority of the population. It is not that the impetus to change or escape from existing conditions is weaker in Britain now than it was a decade and a half earlier. It is simply that many of the existing conditions from which the impetus to escape arises are now associated with the earlier success of socialist policies: a steadily weaker economy, a trade union movement which continues to be disinclined to take the least responsibility for restoring the productive efficiency of this economy and which remains ready to inflict enormous inconvenience on the majority of the population in pursuit of relatively trivial economic gains, a level of effective welfare provision which is already beginning to decline and which will certainly decline drastically further unless the economy can be restored to greater vitality, a series of publicly owned quasi-monopoly providers of goods and services with very limited concern for the convenience of their captive consumers. Not all of these perceptions is, in the round, very just, though none of them is in any sense hallucinatory. But taken together, and even without the adventitious assistance of racial animosities, a rapid increase in violent crime and the excitements of successful foreign military adventure, they make it scarcely surprising that a spirited conservative leadership, even after years of destructive government, should have trounced a divided socialist party which has shifted sharply to the left.

On the whole the main pressure towards socialism has always come from the experience of discontent at the character of an existing society. This is particularly clear in the case of reformist socialism in conditions of free political association and is perhaps disputable in the case of the revolutionary triumphs of socialism. Since the prospects for social revolution depend not merely on the inflamed character of class sentiments or the intensity of immediate class conflict, but also on the analytically distinct domestic strengths and weaknesses of an incumbent state and the external economic, ideological, political and military pressures to which this state is subject,[52] it is at least possible that the potential for socialist revolution may be far higher in a country with relatively quiescent domestic class conflict than it is in one in which class hatred has reached a murderous intensity. Once it is recognized that the prospects for social revolution also depend substantially on the political energy, courage, judgement and skill of candidates for political leadership,[53] the view that domestic class sentiments (and the conditions of practical conflict from which these arise and which they help to reinforce) must necessarily in all historical cases furnish the main pressure towards socialism becomes even less convincing. But what all these exceptions mark is the gap between a socialist political outcome attained as a result of a rational and sustained popular desire for such an outcome and a socialist outcome attained through the more or less intrepid and opportunistic exploitation of historical contingencies. Insofar as the prospects for a socialist outcome need not necessarily depend upon the existing sentiments and perceptions of the majority of a particular population, it need not necessarily prove to be one which the majority has any good reason to desire. Where the main pressures towards socialism do not come from popular discontent at the character of an existing society, but instead derive from the impetus of a vigorously

39

machiavellian exploitation of the historical occasion by an entrepreneurial political leadership, there is no reason at all to see a socialist outcome as in any sense democratic – and by now little reason for confidence (Kampuchea) that it will prove on balance even to be politically benign. This is not, of course, to imply that there is good reason to expect it to be on balance politically malign. The very prominent role given to machiavellian considerations in the politics of Leninism can only be rationalized by presuming that socialist allegiance possesses sacramental qualities which guarantee that those who pledge themselves publicly to it cannot on balance do wrong, a presumption which has been overwhelmingly refuted by experience and which never possessed a shred of rational plausibility. But whereas only a fool or a class consisting largely of fools could view a Leninist leader with categorical trust, real individuals, classes and countries in the course of particular political struggles may well find that they have better reason to trust a Leninist leadership than they do any alternative contender for political power. No fact about the politics of modern states is more important than the fact that popular political choice in all of them all the time is only a choice between options which professional contenders for political power succeed in making available. In this perspective at least, even socialist regimes which originate from the most machiavellian and opportunistic of political ventures through a process of domestic political struggle (as opposed to foreign invasion) will for the most part prove to have come to power because a larger proportion of their populations found themselves able in the last instance to trust the winning political leadership than found themselves able to trust its most effective competitor.[54]

XIX.

The pressure towards socialism within capitalist societies, under the aversive impact of many aspects of the capitalist mode of production, has not, of course, been steady and even throughout their history. Even as a set of popular beliefs and sentiments it has depended upon the development of an understanding (or misunderstanding) of the nature and workings of these societies. The development of this understanding has been the product of a process of intellectual exploration (or mystification) in which the energies of large numbers of minds have been employed over long periods and on behalf of the full range of economic, political and cultural interests extant in these societies. In the process of political struggle itself, interpretations of the implications of these interests have won or lost the credence of great masses of the citizenry. Through doing so, they have come, in practice, in a wide variety of ways to modify the state, society, culture and economy of every capitalist society very markedly indeed. (To establish each and every capitalist society in the first place, it was also necessary for pre-capitalist structures and beliefs to be transformed more or less slowly or painfully through a process of protracted struggle which had many important similarities to that which has taken place within capitalist societies since their inception.) The view that the whole of human history has been a history of class struggles is either a trivial truism or a manifest absurdity. But the view that class struggle, however inchoate and lethargic, is a permanent feature of the life of every capitalist society (and thus far of every *soi-disant* socialist society) is an evident matter of fact. (Socialists are quite right in insisting on the omnipresence of conflicts of class in capitalist societies, though, like anyone else, they may easily misdescribe them badly in particular instances. Where they sometimes err dramatically is in failing to see anything but conflicts of class in such societies.) There may well be (and certainly at present are) capitalist societies in which the great bulk of the industrial working class exhibits a very low level of class consciousness: the United States of America, the Federal Republic of Germany. It may indeed be the case that through time such low levels of class consciousness and the freedom of manoeuvre for private capital which their prevalence makes possible will on balance prove to the advantage of at least the employed members of their industrial working class – Japan, and perhaps again the Federal Republic of Germany, would be plausible examples. It certainly could also be the case, as perhaps in Great Britain over the last few decades, that the defensive power of a strong industrial working class in a not very thriving capitalist economy can pose just as formidable a long-term threat to its own economic interests as a class as it does an immediate threat to the interests of private capital. But it is still necessarily true at each particular point in time that the distribution of gains from production between capital and labour in a capitalist economy has the character of a zero-sum game, in which the gain of the one is the loss of the other. Where the psychic relations between the classes are dominated by envy or indignation there is little prospect of modifying the salience of this perception by considering a longer time-span and a broader range of issues than distribution alone. Envy is widely regarded by philosophers as an irrational motive,[55] and few human beings authentically consider it to be an edifying emotion in itself. But it is scarcely a surprising dispositional product of the workings of a capitalist economy. To see the workings of a market economy in their entirety unflinchingly as a public good, as Hayek for example urges, does not merely require the acceptance of an eminently disputable analysis of economic efficiency. It also requires a level of abstraction from immediate experience which it is scarcely conceivable that the great majority of any population could reach and retain for any great length of time in face of the ebb and flow of envy and disappointment.

It is reasonable, therefore, to see the very substantial gap between the economic structures and systems of social welfare of all relatively advanced capitalist societies today, and the model of a predominantly laissez-faire

41

economy supplemented by the New Poor Law, as a politically natural consequence of popular experience of the workings of capitalist economies, particularly under conditions of universal adult suffrage and free political association. Certainly modern capitalist societies have progressed much less far in this direction than socialists might have hoped – and indeed did hope. Unquestionably the present character of these societies is a gross travesty of a socialist conception of the good. But the direction of the movement itself has, until very recently – if with the major exceptions of Fascism in Italy and National Socialism in Germany – proved remarkably constant. With the privilege of historical hindsight it should not by now be difficult to see either why it has proved so constant or why it has failed to move much further in the same direction.

These are notoriously, the classic preoccupations of European social democracy, a political tendency, or a style of socialist politics, which has taken at least three distinct forms. The first of these, embodied most importantly in the years before 1914 in the party of Marx's collaborator Friedrich Engels, the German SPD, saw the direction of development from capitalism to socialism as guaranteed by the internal dynamics of capitalist production. The party differed considerably in the course of its history on the question of how far political action in general and revolutionary political action in particular was to be a necessary ingredient in carrying through the transformation.[56] But it retained, through the discomfitures of the German Revolution of 1918 and the Weimar Republic, a relatively firm assurance of the certainty (or, at worst, the practical accessibility) of the eventual destination. The second form of social democracy, which has dominated the politics of British labour for the greater part of this century and which has reached its most unequivocal form in the German SPD since the end of the Second World War, has abandoned the presumption that a socialist mode of social and economic organization is in any sense the natural destination for modern capitalist societies, and combined this abandonment, unsurprisingly, with a relatively unforced acceptance of the desirability of many aspects of capitalist social and economic organization. In this version, the version whose claim to represent a form of socialism at all is most often repudiated by other socialists, the view that capitalism is in some degree here to stay is therefore an occasion for relief rather than for despondency. The third form of social democracy is considerably less determinate in its political implications than either of the other two. In particular, it makes no explicit presumption about the immanent dynamics of capitalist society, treating it as an open question whether or not this is in fact fated to transform itself in due course into a predominantly socialist form of society. What marks it out analytically as a form of social democracy, accordingly, is not its assessment of future political probabilities, but a feature of its conception of the political good: the firm insistence that effective political democracy is a precondition for the clear superiority of a socialist over a capitalist mode of production.[57] There is no reason to believe that this is a proviso which Karl Marx himself would have wished to dispute. In all but words, however, it has been comprehensively repudiated on his behalf by the most politically successful of twentieth-century movements which have elected to act in his name.

Because of the causal and ethical elusiveness of the criteria for political democracy,[58] there remains extremely wide disagreement even amongst socialists who consider themselves categorically committed to the value of democracy on just what the necessary and sufficient conditions for its existence should be deemed to be. Some, for example, would wish to go little further than to rescind the prohibition on the existence of organized factions within a monopolistic ruling political party proclaimed at the 10th Congress of the Communist Party of the Soviet Union in 1921.[59] (Certainly the prohibition for those who oppose a prevailing line of policy even to organize their dissent is a sufficient condition for the absence of democracy – and, over all but the shortest periods of time and in all but the direst emergencies, it is likely to prove a sufficient condition for the genesis of all manner of political ills.) Others, like some of the Eurocommunists, accept in effect the entire existing apparatus of capitalist democracy, more or less in accordance with its official self-understanding: the rule of law, free competition for popular suffrage between freely constituted political parties acting freely under the law, access to governmental power solely through constitutional channels and on the basis of freely expressed popular support, and the immediate and uncoerced abandonment of political power whenever the constitutional conditions for its legitimate enjoyment have ceased to exist.

None of these commitments will seem especially impressive displays of political virtue to exponents of the second strand of social democracy; and the more cynical observers of the internal political processes of Eurocommunist parties may be excused for entertaining some doubts over whether these commitments would in fact be discharged according to the letter. It is not unknown, after all, for conservative or liberal politicians to go to some lengths in reinterpreting the requirements of the constitution in the effort to cling on to governmental power. But, at least as a statement of good intentions, the Eurocommunist doctrines do remain of some moment. In particular, they mark an important repudiation of that unlimited entitlement to political opportunism which Leninist parties and governments claim as a matter of right, a presumed entitlement the menace of which can hardly be exaggerated. They also, less encouragingly for socialists, mark a relatively explicit acceptance of the judgement that, for the political opportunity to extend socialist institutions to prove benign in practice, it must be secured through the open and authentic support of the majority of a population; and of a population who will be subjected to the full apparatus of ideological discouragement deployed by the defenders of private capital and who must

43

be induced to lend and maintain their support under the severely disadvantageous competitive conditions of a capitalist society in operation. Because the handicaps imposed by these conditions have long been, and because they will assuredly remain, so very acute, the political temptation to bypass democratic procedures has been and will continue to be a very strong one. (The degree of Marx's own commitment to democratic values in the course of political struggle did not merely vacillate in the face of practical opportunities;[60] it also depended in the last instance on his presumption that the laws of motion of capitalist society were already beginning to form and would inevitably in the long run succeed in forming a solidary and self-conscious majority of support for the establishment and maintenance of a socialist polity.) What the experience of twentieth-century politics has most decisively shown is that in those societies which already politically have much to lose, the liberal democracies of advanced capitalism, any deliberate attempt to subvert democratic procedures in the quest for socialism is an act of reckless adventurism. (The position would obviously be very different even in advanced capitalist societies in the course of a war in which their own legal governments had fallen and their territories had succumbed to enemy occupation; and in decidedly less advanced capitalist societies which do not at the time enjoy any form of democratic government whatever, it is yet more different still.) This third version of social democracy, therefore, despite the vagueness of its commitments and perhaps the vagueness with which it has so far been described here, does at least plainly assert the dependence, for the populations of the liberal democracies of advanced capitalism, of the desirability of any transition to socialism on a road to power which does not flout or assail existing constitutional forms.

The most evocative attacks on this restriction, which must certainly be recognized as a substantial inhibition in any socialist quest for power, come from socialists who wish to insist upon the need to maintain more exigent criteria for democracy. They need not deny, and if they are at all historically discerning they will not deny, that the institutions of liberal capitalist democracies are in some measure democratic. But they will point, in contrast to the sovereign popular assemblies of the Greek polis or Lenin's prophecies in *State and Revolution*, to many respects in which the economic, political and social orders of every modern capitalist state are very imperfectly democratic indeed. A strategy for moving towards democracy, in their eyes, will predominantly take the form of seeking to democratize component institutions of these societies. Particularly, it will seek to sustain the genuinely democratic character of the political party which undertakes to lead the struggle for socialism within them, and to organize in the aftermath of political triumph the socialist societies which will succeed them. It is the intensity of commitment to this goal, the purity of political will which this intensity of commitment makes possible, and the transparently democratic

44

qualities of the party which exemplifies this purity of will, which are to be the practical guarantees of the benignity of this strategy. In the light of these guarantees, any serious measure of inhibition in the face of what obviously remain massively imperfect democratic routines in the incumbent states will show a bovine fetishism of the evaluative terminology affected by the defenders of private capital, rather than a prudent sensitivity to the perils of authoritarian politics.

As a critical commentary on the optimism or selective inattention of exponents of the third form of social democracy, this line of thought has a good deal of force. But it is not in itself politically altogether benign. It is, for example, excessively disposed to take the will for the deed; and it unduly neglects the extent to which even the Bolshevik Party, both in its conception of the political good itself and of the form of society which was to embody this and to furnish the eventual political reward of its struggles, in fact shared the radically democratic model on which it sets such store. The temptation to take the will for the deed is one to which all political actors are subject. (To be utterly incapable of so doing would, after all, be to be deprived of any reason to act politically at all.) But both the degree to which political actors, singly or in organized bodies, succeed in assessing accurately the consequences of their actions, and the degree to which they contrive to deceive themselves over the likely consequences of their actions, vary enormously. To misjudge the probable consequences of seeking to institutionalize a particular understanding of political value can be of immense political importance. A sympathetic view of the life and thought of Lenin, for example, might see this, and all that has followed from it, as the working through of just such a spectacular error of judgement.[61] The radically democratic conception of the political good possesses considerable attractions; at least for those for whom it possesses any attraction at all. But they are the attractions of ethical stipulation rather than those of proven institutional design. There is every reason to doubt whether a large human organization engaged in a tense struggle to master a refractory human environment could in fact exemplify such ethical stipulations with any consistency for any great length of time – the temptations to do otherwise for many of its members being so intense and the political difficulty of inducing others to continue to resist them being so acute. (Political leadership, it must be remembered, is a competitive activity. Political leaders who reject too many enticing opportunities, even for the most virtuous of reasons, are apt to find themselves removed by their irritated followers.) There is still more reason to doubt whether any such organization could prove at all effective in political conflict if it did succeed in exemplifying these ethical stipulations at all consistently. Both the historical experience of participatory democracy in the Greek polis and the theoretical arguments of Jean-Jacques Rousseau strongly suggest that a high degree of democracy requires a relatively low level of mutual risk amongst the members of the demos and a scope of political conflict restricted by a comparatively narrow range of divisions of interest. In the necessarily bitter struggle to transform capitalist into socialist societies, the inhibitions of a radically democratic hostility to the concentration of authority and initiative are likely in practice to appear, and indeed to be, absurdly high. Hence the likelihood that any commitment to such inhibitions will sooner or later, when it most matters, turn out to be in bad faith: to have become purely verbal. An authentic and consistent commitment to radical democracy in this context will almost certainly prove simply a recipe for political ineffectiveness. There is, after all, a real danger that even the less extreme commitment to respect the constitutional routines of liberal democratic states will prove to be a recipe for being politically ineffective. But since the inhibitions accepted in this second case are less extreme and far easier to identify clearly, there is at least more prospect that they can be accepted and maintained consistently amidst the dangers and acrimonies of practical politics.

XX.

If the inhibitions of social democracy, in this understanding, are accepted firmly, it is particularly important to assess the balance of political pressures which arises from the nature of advanced capitalist societies as these are today and as they are likely to become in the reasonably near future. The actual prospects for major political change in such societies today certainly depend upon the dynamics of the world economy and of the geopolitical competition between nation states at least as much as they do on the conflict of domestic social forces. But the acceptance of a democratic form of socialist transformation is essentially a commitment to eschew the chance opportunities for exploiting internal instabilities thrown up by these turmoils, in favour of a comparatively transparent and internally responsible mode of political agency. Accordingly, one of the most important presumptions of this version of social democracy is the dual judgement that no socialist political agency in what is initially an operating capitalist democracy can deserve to exercise power unless it can convince the majority of its electorate (under the prevailing electoral system) that it does deserve to do so and that no socialist political agency will in fact contrive to exercise power in such a state unless it is in fact clearly judged to deserve to do so by the majority of its electorate. It is quite possible that this last judgement is incorrect. But the greater the probability of its proving *in extremis* to be incorrect, the more damaging in the eyes of most of the electorate will be a clear political disposition to act unconstitutionally, should the opportunity arise, to a political party under less extreme circumstances. Even if it might be advantageous, therefore, to retain the will and capacity to act quite ruthlessly in the face of special opportunities, it will be indispensable under all circumstances to *appear* rigorously committed to the observance of democratic constraints.[62] Hence Eurocommunism.

Is there any reason to believe that the internal political pressures towards collectivism, which stem from the experience for the majority of its population of what it is like to live in a capitalist society, are now beginning to slacken? Should we now expect these to be replaced by countervailing pressures for an extension and deepening of market relations? There are certainly some reasons for taking this view. There is first, and not altogether trivially, the very extensive electoral success across the capitalist world, in the face of major recession, of parties dedicated to the defence and revitalization of capitalist production firmly conceived as such. There is secondly the evidence of resistance to the levels of direct taxation on personal incomes which are required to fund the existing levels of public welfare provision in advanced capitalist societies (on top, to be sure, of their huge expenditures on defence). There is thirdly a pronounced absence of enthusiasm amongst the populace at large and amongst professional economists for the monopolistic or semi-monopolistic state corporation's capacity to act as an efficient and consumer-responsive producer of goods or provider of services. Perhaps most importantly of all, and particularly in the weaker capitalist economies in the face of recession, there is a growing conviction that the social democratic welfare states amongst advanced capitalist societies set a political priority on distribution over production which has by now become self-evidently harmful. One major reason for construing all these as significant modifications of the internal dynamics of advanced capitalist societies is that each of them is a product of fairly extended popular experience of actual modifications of these societies in a socialist direction. Part of the internal dynamic of advanced capitalism, that is to say, is by now an aversive response to the experience of socialist institutions.

In addition, there are a number of other aspects of social, economic and cultural change in these societies which have weakened or are weakening the political power and confidence of socialist forces. Some of these are extremely crude, if not necessarily very lasting. The crudest of all is the huge increase in long-term unemployment and the sharp contraction, in particular, in the numbers of industrial workers and of service and quasi-intellectual workers employed by the public sector. The existence of mass unemployment and the threat of its further extension do not merely weaken the organized working class in wage bargaining and in the general capacity to defend its interests at work, they also markedly lower its self-assurance, vitality and solidarity throughout the field of politics. In particular, they further cripple what little confidence the class has succeeded in mustering in

47

its capacity to carry through the destiny, assigned to it by Marx, of assuming and discharging responsibility for the process of production itself. The sharp rise in unemployment has accelerated the slow decomposition of traditional working-class communities, thinned the ranks of industrial workers and cut drastically into the membership of trade unions. In Britain at least, it has left a political movement of the organized working class, which had long been rationally confident, at least of its overwhelming capacities for effective obstruction, uneasily aware of being based in a potentially shrinking past and not in a securely expanding future. Somewhat more elusively, this collective wilting in the broadly socialist self-confidence of the organized working class has been accompanied, and in some measure preceded, by a relatively acute and widespread cultural mutation in attitudes towards the meaning of work itself. This is not a well-described process, and its causes are not at all well understood. But it has been very widely noted and its political importance is very great. The simplest and commonest characterization of this mutation is the refusal to attach any dignity whatever to labour itself, an insistence on the claims of a wholly irresponsible personal licence and a more or less comprehensively nihilist refusal to treat organized social relations (including relations of production) as a focus of value. Opinions differ over how far this development is to be seen as cultural disaster and how far as political promise.[64] But it seems reasonably clear that it does represent in the first instance both a cultural disaster and a practical political menace to any scheme of socialist politics founded upon the political assurance and cultural solidarity of an organized industrial working class. A combination of apathetic and apolitical privatization amongst the great majority of the youthful unemployed with sporadic outbreaks of anomic violence will hardly pose a formidable political challenge to a confident right-wing government already all too disposed to enhance its capacities for domestic repression wherever this proves necessary.

There is no reason, therefore, to regard the faltering of even the most tentatively socialist politics in most of the advanced capitalist world in the early 1980s as a meaningless political mishap, let alone as essentially illusory. But neither is there the least reason to assume that the aversive pressures of capitalist relations of production are somehow fading away. What certainly has proved true, however, is that the variety of more or less socialist political agencies inherited from the past have in most cases recently proved highly ineffective, either in assessing the forms in which these aversive pressures are currently experienced, or in suggesting at all convincingly how they might effectively be alleviated. There is every reason, that is to say, to treat the recent (though in no sense historically unprecedented) failures of socialist politics as just that: failures in socialist *politics*.

XXI.

In the domestic politics of advanced capitalist societies the pressures towards socialism (the socialization of production and the egalitarian rectification of the distributive consequences of founding an economy on market exchange) will continue to come in the future, as they have in the past, from the aversive stimuli of anarchic production and from the large and arbitrary inequalities which this generates. In conditions of high and durable unemployment, there is every reason to expect these pressures to increase rather than diminish. With the dramatic changes in labour utilization which must follow recent technological change, particularly in the processing of information, there is every reason to anticipate a continuance of high levels of unemployment even in most of the more robust advanced capitalist economies. In the less robust advanced capitalist economies, like Great Britain, it is hard by now to see how a purely market adaptation of the economy to these novel competitive conditions could be carried through without the most catastrophic consequences for a large proportion of the population – many millions of people. (Only a socialist party manifestly unfit to take responsibility for adapting the national economy could readily have lost a national election in Great Britain in the summer of 1983.) What is virtually certain, therefore, about advanced capitalist economies in the relatively near future is that they will continue to provide, and that most of them will be perceived by very many of their inhabitants as continuing to provide, occasions for major socialist reforms. Hence, for example, the electoral success even in the midst of deep recession of socialist parties in Sweden and France. It does not follow from this, and it might conceivably not prove to be the case in practice, that the majority of such societies will be more socialist in their institutions and economic structures in three decades' time, even in the absence of major nuclear war, than they are at present. But what does follow is that whether or not particular advanced capitalist countries move in this direction over these decades will depend quite largely on the political intelligence and skill of exponents of socialism within them.

Political skill has many dimensions; but in this instance its most important dimension will be the ability to identify, and to express convincingly, the superior capacity of socialist institutions or expedients to handle particular problems of these societies. There are plainly a number of distinct necessary conditions for demonstrating this ability, the most important of which is that there should actually be some problems in these societies which socialist institutions or expedients do possess a superior capacity to handle. Comparing the Great Britain of 1983 with that of 1834, or indeed 1900, it is reasonably apparent that in the past such superior capacity has certainly existed, though critics of socialism would naturally wish to add that the cost of the unintended consequences of these improvements has been far higher than socialists care to admit. A second necessary condition, of a more crudely political variety, is that socialist political leaders should succeed in identifying and in giving convincing expression to the particular superior capacities which socialism does continue to enjoy. To be successful in this task they need by now not merely to possess a keen eye for the discontents which result from capitalist relations themselves, but also an equally keen eye for those which today arise from existing socialist institutions and expedients within their own society. An unreassuring habit of exponents of socialist politics is that, while they find it easy enough to envisage political competition itself, where the criteria of skill are highly elusive, as a game of skill, they nevertheless find it quite natural to describe the socialist exercise of governmental power, because of the supposed simplicity and rationality of its purposes and because of its manifestly good intentions, as a virtually automatic process of beneficence.

The most serious political doubt about socialist policies in advanced capitalist societies, a doubt now massively grounded in the experience of the populations of these societies wherever socialist politics has had any real success, is whether socialist governments do or can know what they are doing. It is a doubt about the cognitive and practical coherence of socialist government. The only effective way of laying this doubt to rest is a convincing display of the possession of causal understanding: the frank acknowledgement that there have been large and important unintended consequences of applying socialist expedients in the past and the open proposal of carefully considered and clearly described measures for avoiding or ameliorating such consequences in the future. The simple hope that the attention of enough of the populace will wander from these deficiencies at the next electoral occasion is not only an ignoble (or corrupt) basis on which to seek governmental power, it is also a fairly effective guarantee that the chances of obtaining power will be reduced to a minimum and that its acquisition and exercise, should this nevertheless occur, will once again prove to have deeply discouraging results. Even if such an attitude does not yield the disastrous short-term consequences which it richly deserves, it can hardly fail to yield even more disastrous consequences in the somewhat longer run. A capitalist liberal democracy does not leave much power in the hands of its citizens. (What modern state does?) But it leaves enough to guarantee that systematic political irresponsibility will sooner or later be found out and punished.

XXII.

There are two very different ways of looking at the experience of living in an advanced capitalist society, one of which is determinedly objective and the other of which is quite confessedly subjective in its focus. Any attempt to consider the future prospects for socialism in these countries must do its best to keep them as distinct as possible. The first, the objective, is a relatively determinate matter. It emphasizes the effective entitlements to economic goods and services, brought about by the working of the private capital and labour markets, state fiscal and monetary agencies and public welfare provision, and guaranteed directly by the legal structure and coercive power of the state. This system of entitlements is linked strongly and dynamically to the workings of the world economy which ensures that many aspects of it will be reshaped constantly by forces acting from outside the territorial borders of the state. It is a common trick of contemporary political vision and sentiment to view the domestic structure of effective entitlements at any one time as a wholly legitimate collective asset, to be reassigned at discretion in accordance with the collective moral taste of the populace, and to view the external linkages of this system to the world economy as its exposure to unmoralized and at best weakly controllable foreign force. There is something to be said for each of these conceptions, but nothing whatever for their bland combination: since affirming the categories on which one depends requires the contradiction of the categories on which the other depends. On the whole it is analytically most helpful to view the entire system of entitlements, internally and internationally, as both a structure of powers and a field of power. In all advanced capitalist societies (even the United States of America) the level of domestic entitlements now depends to a considerable degree upon the external linkages of the economy. In Great Britain this dependence has long been particularly deep; and its present implications are dramatically alarming. In any advanced capitalist society the population has good reason to assess the immediate charms of socialist projects for domestic redistribution in the light of their only slightly less immediate implications for the international competitiveness of its economy. In an economy with the striking external competitive weakness of the present British economy, the prospective impact of a government's policies on the international competitiveness of the economy is the most important single consideration facing the population.[65]

There are at least two indispensable elements to such policies. One is a coherent and potentially effective policy for the conduct of international trade. The second is a politically realistic proposal for a means of rapidly raising the share of investment in the gross national product and rapidly diminishing in compensation the share of current consumption. No socialist party which lacked such policies (or which ludicrously promised to combine them with unfettered wage bargaining throughout the economy) could have any serious claim to be fit to rule Great Britain at present. There is certainly some doubt, both in principle and in practice, as to the technical efficiency of socialist investment agencies. But in a society with a pattern of class sentiments and a structure of organized class forces like Great Britain's, it seems extremely likely that any more unequivocally capitalist method of

51

shifting resources from consumption to investment will be enormously more wasteful in strictly economic terms and will involve much more violent social conflict (if indeed, in the end, it could be carried through at all). There clearly is, therefore, an opportunity in Britain at present for a socialist project for major economic changes designed to restore the international competitiveness of the economy. There is an overwhelming popular interest in such restoration, since it is certainly a necessary condition for sustaining, let alone improving, the purely economic standard of living of the great majority of the population. But to be able to take this opportunity and to carry through the necessary reconstruction would require a party with the clarity of judgement to see the need, the honesty to acknowledge it and the political prowess to win and hold the loyalty of (at least) the industrial working class in carrying through this reconstruction. (It would also, of course, require a practical policy for carrying it through which would actually work.) At present in Britain no political party comes anywhere near meeting this standard; and the economic prospects of the majority of the population – and the longer-term social and political prospects of the population as a whole – are correspondingly ugly.

XXIII.

The second way of envisaging the experience of living in an advanced capitalist society, the subjective way, would consider this as a structure of meanings and significances for individual persons and sets of persons, and not merely as a structure of effective entitlements to material goods and economic services. It is a cultural rather than an economic perspective. As such it lacks the insistence and the relative determinacy of outline of the latter, implying more nebulous criteria for success and failure and far weaker differentiation between capitalist and socialist social arrangements. It would be absurd, for the most delicate of sensibilities, to treat it as enjoying priority over, or even causal equivalence with, the strictly economic structure. But it would be equally absurd to regard it as politically inconsequential in contrast with the latter – or indeed to deny the direct causal impact which it exerts upon this in motivating the cooperation or obstruction of particular economic actors.

It is true that Marx himself presumed that a socialist mode of economic production would mark a clear economic advance on any capitalist mode, ending alienation in the labour process, abolishing the anarchy of production, terminating domestic class conflict and enabling the forces of production to continue to expand without avoidable impediments. It is also true that not merely Lenin but also Stalin, Khrushchev and presumably even Andropov continued firmly to credit this assumption. But it is clear by now that a socialist mode of production, whether or not it is indeed a necessary condition for each of these improvements, is some way from being a sufficient condition for any of them.[66] It is still in some measure an open question whether socialist production as such is, on balance, more or less efficient than capitalist production.[67] But what is no longer in doubt is that it has a large number of intrinsic sources of major inefficiency of its own and that there are as yet no proven socialist expedients for eliminating most of these. As a result, there has been a substantial number of major retreats from more socialist to more capitalist modes of economic organization within socialist states: in the USSR in the 1920s, in Yugoslavia in the 1950s, in Hungary in the 1960s, in rural China in the early 1980s. But for the external military guarantee of the Soviet army, there is every reason to suppose that the political and economic pressures which produced these movements would have worked themselves through more uniformly and perhaps decidedly further at least in all the socialist states of Eastern Europe.

Moreover, there is little reason to credit the limited degree to which the societies of advanced capitalism have been modified in a socialist direction to the operation of narrowly economic pressures. The disfigurements of capitalism are both more realistically seen and more consistently experienced as cultural as well as purely economic blemishes. The political response to capitalism inside the democracies of the West has been as consistently a response to cultural as it has to strictly economic discontents. Furthermore, except in the provision of minimum welfare, it has been far more successful as a response to cultural discontents than it has to economic ones. Even such prominent socialist political purposes as economic redistribution are best understood as cultural as much as economic goals. The conjunction of huge aggregations of inherited personal wealth with the ugly and alarming conditions in which millions still have to live is far more important as a cultural affront than it is as an economic injury. The redistribution of all substantial aggregations of private wealth in a society like Britain (or even the United States) would make a relatively trivial once and for all contribution to the material welfare of the great majority. But to live in a society which contrived to preserve all the other merits of these countries, but which no longer set off the distress of their less fortunate members by the gross luxury of a tiny parasitic class would at least make it easier to see the society itself as a single community and membership within it as a human bond with some genuine moral significance. It is extremely difficult to ascertain just how most of their members do regard extreme social inequality,[68] and no doubt reasonable to assume that their attitudes are in large measure vague and confused. But at least in a country with the historical class experiences and current class perceptions of Great Britain, there is every reason to see the cultural affront as politically important and to see its removal or diminution as a necessary condition for the large measure of voluntary delayed gratification on the part of the organized working class (amongst others) which would be a necessary condition for seriously improving the economy.

In cultural terms at least, the prospect of a capitalist economy permanently unable to supply a large proportion of the society's adult members with gainful employment is not a pretty one. What sense can such victims be expected to make of their membership of a society which remains complacently or maliciously capitalist in its values? What resources are there in the tradition of self-understanding of capitalist production for lending significance to any such fate? What resources are there for taking the human opportunities furnished by the increasing availability and economic superiority of a massively capital-intensive and labour-displacing technology to reorganize the work, lives and existential opportunities of a population in a way which genuinely attaches an equal value to all the members of the society (not as prospective creators, but simply as persons with a life to live)? It should not, unfortunately, be assumed that socialist thought and action necessarily possesses at present any very powerful and precise set of expedients for dealing with these challenges either. Its past ventures in the cultural modification of a society like Britain have had many consequences which were as unintended as they have proved unfortunate. The relation amongst the relatively young in Britain at present between attitudes to work, work opportunities, cultural values and the guarantee of minimum public welfare provision is not an encouraging one (even for a socialist who would not care to applaud the presence of the Puritan apothegm: 'He who does not work, neither shall he eat' in the constitution of the USSR).[69] The attempt to establish an unselective public educational system at the secondary level for the entire remainder of the population (while preserving the charitable status of the Public Schools) – in its own terms a strikingly simple, if mildly confused, attempt to express the value of egalitarian solidarity – has done little or nothing to improve the worst schools in the country, but has effectively excluded the ablest of working-class children from the outstanding educational opportunities to which a modest proportion of them previously had access.

Perhaps most disastrous of all has been the record of post-war British immigration policy and its consequences. On this matter no figure in British public life has consistently shown insight, honesty and scruple. Through a curious combination of anomalies in British nationality law left by the decomposition of empire, paternalist commitments to former imperial subjects, brief passages of humanitarian concern for persecuted groups abroad, intermittent demand for fresh supplies of unskilled labour, belated acknowledgement of responsibility to what were now resident British citizens, more or less intense political cowardice and the almost limitless incapacity to grasp what was occurring, Great Britain has acquired an array of racial animosities which virtually no element in the society can soberly regard with equanimity. More recently, of course, it has also been offered a handful of draconic political remedies for this predicament, involving more or less voluntary mass deportation. But even if the remedies were less barbarous or better motivated, there is no shadow of a doubt of their practical inadequacy to the occasions for which they are offered. In a capitalist society in deep economic crisis, with massive unemployment, deep divisions of interest within the working class and an increasingly threatened and hysterical sense of national self-regard, this pattern of immigration could hardly in principle have failed to distress and harm the interests of a substantial section of the indigenous working class (there is no large immigrant population at Chatsworth), and to leave to a large proportion of the immigrants themselves a miserable range of economic options and an ugly and protracted experience of semi-overt persecution and communal animosity.

It was not, in retrospect, at all a good idea. But it came about, in part at least, through the exercise of what were thought and felt at the time to be the very best of intentions. Because of the retrospective folly of this trajectory and the savagely damaging discretion with which it has been assessed and described in public for most of its course, there is virtually no element in British society today which comes out of it with much honour, though all too evidently some sections of British society, both indigenous and immigrant, have suffered (and will continue to suffer) enormously more from it than others. It would be misleading to explain the trajectory in its entirety in terms of effective demand for labour on a capitalist labour market.[70] But it would be reasonable to attribute some of the discretion, and almost all of the more creditable aspects of the socialist response, both in trade unions and in the Labour Party, to a commitment, at least a verbal commitment, to the cosmopolitan solidarity of labour. There are certainly some cultural problems of advanced capitalist societies today for which socialist remedies, however theoretically beguiling, have proved in practice impossibly difficult to apply.[71]

XXIV.

A socialist society aspires to distribute labour tasks and opportunities, and effective entitlements to economic goods, on the basis of egalitarian communal membership; and it hopes to succeed in doing so without militating against the productivity of labour and the resulting range and scale of effective economic entitlements. The hope that such an egalitarian basis of distribution will be genuinely accepted in practice and that it will not sharply diminish the production of material goods is essentially a cultural hope.

55

Where, in an economy in which the means of production are publicly owned, the cultural hope proves to have been over-optimistic, economic productivity is sustained in practice (insofar as it is sustained) not only by a more divisive system of material incentives, but also by the effective prohibition of opportunities for the self-organization of labour and by a high level of purely political oppression. To implement such cultural hopes, without damage to a capitalist economy strongly linked to the world market, in the face of free and powerful labour organizations and within the political framework of a liberal democratic state, would be an extraordinary political accomplishment. (It would require, amongst many other things, the enthusiastic and skilful cooperation of huge numbers of people in wildly heterogeneous practical situations.) The cultural and political force of pressures for a more equitable and morally plausible basis for allocating economic opportunities and sacrifices over the next few decades in capitalist societies are therefore likely not to support but to militate against attempts within the weaker capitalist economies to restore or maintain the purely economic efficacy of these economies. The intuitive cultural plausibility of socialist remedies for the former problems is likely to be offset by the culturally repulsive features of any serious remedies for the latter ones. Since the latter are in any case extremely difficult to address directly (and since in at least some capitalist economies they will scarcely be resolved successfully), the political temptation to concentrate upon the former and to ignore the latter for as long as possible will continue to be acute.

There are definitely a number of types of large-scale human organization – armies, hospitals, blood banks[72] – which are not most effectively organized on the basis of a competitive response by individuals to narrowly material incentives. (It is in fact extremely unlikely that there are *any* large-scale human organizations which could operate successfully *solely* on the basis of such incentives.) But the aspiration to replace material by moral incentives throughout the productive system of a society has received little encouragement from the experience of socialist production. Since the history of theoretical enthusiasm for ascetic and economically egalitarian participatory communities extends back long before the emergence of any predominantly capitalist society, it is clear that the appeals of such communities (for those who find them appealing) cannot simply be an artefact of popular revulsion from the experience of capitalist production. But insofar as these appeals have ever become at all widespread in any modern society,[73] it is reasonable to presume that they have derived their force from the aversive impact of capitalist inequalities and arbitrarinesses, and that little if any of this force has come from any zest for asceticism as such. (It is reasonable, that is to say, to presume not merely that Adam Smith and David Hume were right to see modern commercial society as uniquely effective at improving the real standard of living of the majority of the population, but also that the subsequent political viability of capitalism has been in large measure a result of its capacity to continue to expand production and to extend the consumption opportunities of the majority.) If socialism is at all widely supposed to mean a diminution of, or a narrowing in, the consumption opportunities of the majority (as the defenders of private capital will certainly attempt to cause it to be seen), this is likely to prove a formidable obstacle to its further extension. The most dismaying fear about socialism in this context would be that its evident cultural appeals are radically parasitic upon capitalist production and incapable of surviving the demise of the latter: that an economy founded on justice and a very modest level of mutual benevolence (let alone one conceived as a system of mutual service) would not merely work very poorly and lower the standard of living to which the majority of the populations of advanced capitalist societies have become accustomed (or, perhaps, had until very recently become accustomed), but that it would also in practice come to be so cordially detested that it could be kept in operation only by a high level of political repression, of commands backed by threats.

The cultural pressures towards socialism have naturally not been uniform in strength from one capitalist society to another or from one decade to another within the same capitalist society. (In the United States of America, notoriously, and for reasons which are still rather opaque, these pressures have for the most part proved particularly weak.) In the 1950s and 1960s the presumption that the aversive cultural pressures towards socialism in advanced capitalist societies had weakened dramatically or even virtually petered out became quite widespread. Yet the reasons given for crediting this verdict were never very impressive. In the light of subsequent experience it seems reasonable to conclude that, although in the face of an abundance of bread and circuses the levels of popular animosity towards capitalist ownership can become quite low, and can remain quite low for long periods of time, the potentiality for cultural revulsion from capitalist ownership is simply inseparable from this. In countries which combine weak capitalist economies and consequently erratic provision of bread, circuses, or even work opportunities, with relatively strong political traditions of hostility towards capitalism, such cultural revulsion can be expected to remain not merely vigorous but also politically of considerable importance. The key political issue for such societies, accordingly, is how far this revulsion can be put politically to a sound and well-considered use. To put it to such use requires a political party which does not merely give resonant expression to the revulsion itself but also contrives to employ the power, political commitment and popular flexibility which it draws from this resonant expression to reorganize economic and social roles in the society in ways which work more satisfactorily. Because the most important criterion of satisfactory working is bound, over time, to be the productive efficacy of the economy within the international trading system – there are no productively very effective modern autarkies – and because the feelings which such a government would express (and on which it would continue to depend for much of its power) consort so uncomfortably with the causal requirements for productive efficacy, it would require immense political skill to transpose even fervent popular enthusiasm into effective economic policies. No party which neglected in advance even to explain to its members or to the electorate at large precisely how it hoped to carry through this transposition would stand the least chance of success in doing so. (And any party which did neglect to do this would thereby be indicating political intentions which were at best frivolous and at worst dishonest and vicious.)

A socialist party which concentrated its attention on the cultural disfigurements of capitalism might on occasion stand an excellent chance of winning governmental power – though it would stand less chance of doing so, even against an incumbent government whose economic policies had proved blatantly disastrous, at the hands of an electorate already rationally acutely anxious about the fate of the economy. What such a socialist party could not hope to accomplish would be to achieve any very durable success in diminishing the disfigurements of capitalism. In the end, at least in any society in which the populace at large enjoys some real measure of political choice, competitors for governmental power who can plausibly claim the capacity to rescue a faltering economy will have the edge on those who prefer to ignore its travails or who offer as remedies what are transparently nothing more than placebos.

If the cultural offensiveness of capitalism continues, despite Marx, to furnish the main source of political pressure within capitalist societies for their modification in a socialist direction, the extent to which such modification is carried through in practice will continue to be determined through political competition. Both David Hume and Friedrich von Hayek have acknowledged that capitalist relations of ownership and right are a politically sustained artifice, often at odds with many natural emotional and moral responses of human beings. Hayek certainly sees the political task of defending capitalism in the face of the more or less systematic cultural revulsion which has stemmed from these responses as considerably more taxing than Hume realized that it would prove.[74] But he also sees the indispensability of such defence for securing the productive advantages of a capitalist order in even starker terms than those of Hume or Smith. It remains a highly contentious question just how far the productive advantages of capitalism do require its cultural disfigurements – how far, for example, restrictions upon the inheritance of private wealth or upon gifts *inter vivos*, redistributive taxation, public welfare provision and the expansion of a quasi-monopolistic or at worst semi-parasitic public sector, impair the allocative efficiency of capital and labour markets, or the economic and cultural incentives of entrepreneurs or workers. In some cases, such as the public provision of high-quality education (a facility certainly favoured by Adam Smith himself), or health care, any such strictly economic incompatibility is singularly implausible. On the other hand, the presumption that a redistributive tax system will not at any point prove to have severely negative effects on the productive incentives of real human beings in real societies (capitalist or socialist) can hardly be reconciled with the immense energies devoted to tax evasion in the former or the huge transfers of labour power from legal to illegal economic activities in both.

XXV.

The extent to which capitalist societies do become transformed in a socialist direction will continue, therefore, to be determined through political struggle. In that struggle the skill and nerve of political actors and the more or less idiosyncratic history of class sentiment within particular societies will continue to play a major role; and the outcome will continue to be affected powerfully by economic, military and even ideological pressures exerted from outside the particular capitalist society in question. But the main ideological weight in the political struggle is likely to go on resting on the proven cultural deformations of capitalism and on the increasingly evident political and economic hazards of socialism. (It would also, of course, be affected dramatically by a sudden collapse of the entire world capitalist economy, as a result of a major banking crisis or large-scale war. But it would be rash, on past experience, to expect these conditions politically to favour socialist expedients any more handsomely than political competition under circumstances of modest prosperity.)

Two final points require emphasis. The first is that socialists have every reason, on the basis of their own beliefs, to expect this struggle on occasion to become extremely violent. Even a conception of the transition to socialism which sees this in essence as a slow pacific process of cognitive and moral advance can hardly exclude from its full realization, in however tactful a form, the expropriation of the expropriators. This is not an outcome which the expropriators themselves can be expected to welcome. Since a socialist understanding of the character of this transition sees it in the last instance as a process of more or less muted civil war, socialists ought not to be surprised if their enemies at times prove to act with extreme ruthlessness. On a socialist understanding, such action *in extremis* may well be perfectly rational. (*Cet animal est très méchant. Quand on l'attaque, il se défend.*) Unsuccessful revolutionary ventures are apt to be appallingly costly;[75] and even predominantly reformist and essentially democratic socialist governments can find themselves overthrown with great brutality. The moral of such hazards is not that they can usually or even often be forestalled by the adoption of a more swashbuckling and aggressive style of socialist politics,[76] nor that any attempt at political improvement is to be eschewed since it may always end in tears. (The same is true in spades of the decision to avoid all effort at political improvement.) It is simply that any theoretical and practical conception of the merits of socialist development must take careful account of the prospect of the more or less intense resistance which this development is likely to encounter. The political theory of socialism is obliged to consider such development not as a consummation devoutly to be wished (an ideally desirable social and political order), but as a political goal which can rationally and morally be sought in definite ways in real societies and at particular times. It is not an external and accidental feature of the struggle for socialism that it carries high risks and can under some circumstances elicit political reactions of extreme barbarism. Any defensible policy of socialist struggle must attend to such risks throughout, seek to hold them to a minimum and adjust its strategy in their face with the utmost prudence. If it happened to be clearly true that most ventures in socialist transformation ended in a repressive bloodbath, this would not necessarily in any way impugn the claims of socialism to represent an ideally desirable political order. But it would make the active pursuit of socialist politics on other than religious grounds extremely hard to defend. (Of course, if it happened to be clearly true that all ventures in socialist transformation inevitably end in a repressive bloodbath, it would merely make such ventures deranged. The lust for self-destruction is definitely *not* a creative lust.)

The second point is equally banal but perhaps less discouraging. Since the principal practical difficulty of socialist politics is the construction of political institutions and organizations which combine efficacy with trustworthiness, the conditions of political struggle within a capitalist democracy may in many ways be particularly propitious for socialist politics. It is certainly true that the institutional structures of such a state offer formidable obstructive advantages to the defenders of private capital and the privileges which go with this. But some of these obstructive advantages derive from institutional provisions which socialism itself certainly requires in some form and which indeed it promises in due course to extend and strengthen (the rule of law, freedom of speech and political association, a measure of civil rights, a government genuinely responsible to those whom it governs).[77] Many of these advantages are not merely presumptive adornments of an eventual socialist destination, they are also potential advantages in the meantime to any reasonably substantial socialist political advance. Genuinely to accept constitutional restraints might on occasion imply the loss of real political opportunities. But to accept the need to construct a political organization which not only succeeds in securing, but actually *deserves*, the trust of its popular following is more likely to augment than to diminish the political prospects for socialism.

Democratic socialism as a political practice

The pragmatic political importance of securing the active trust and commitment of the working class as a whole has been a prominent theme of socialist political theory in the West since the Second World War. The *locus classicus* of its expression is the analysis of the basis of the political power of private capital within western states offered some decades earlier by the Italian Marxist Antonio Gramsci. Gramsci's conception of hegemony identifies the political dominance of private capital in the West as a product of ideological improvisation and incorporation at least as much as of simple repressive force.[78] As the institutional structures of the democratic capitalist state indeed require, the sustaining of capitalist relations of production in these states depends upon the relatively active belief of a substantial proportion (perhaps even a majority) of the population that these relations are either practically indispensable or essentially desirable in themselves: that there exists no morally or prudentially acceptable alternative to them. In these societies, where the state itself is not a detached instrument of control in the hands of a determinate group of persons and potentially open to sudden seizure under tactically advantageous conditions, but instead depends intimately and elaborately on the active energies of civil society, the basis of political power does rest largely (as David Hume presumed it always must)[79] upon opinion. In this setting, therefore, the struggle for political power takes the form of a struggle to shape and dominate belief and sentiment, to establish what Gramsci called 'hegemony'. Simply as a strategic appreciation this assessment has held up very well. Political efficacy for a socialist party within the competitive arena of a capitalist democracy requires the nurturing and reinforcement in a popular following of a vision of the character and significance of the society sharply at odds with that favoured (and very extensively propagated) by the defenders of private capital. The more extensive the socialist transformation aspired to, the more urgent the need to fashion and extend an alternative understanding of the defects of the existing society and the real possibilities for their rectification. Since socialists are not the only ones capable of abandoning constitutional routines when they judge such abandonment to be to their advantage,[80] the fullest attainable extension of socialist perceptions and evaluations throughout civil society is not merely the most promising approach to the task of mustering and retaining a substantial electoral allegiance, it is also and at least equally importantly the best protection available to a socialist party in the ascendant against the sudden abrogation of a liberal democratic constitution by the defenders of a beleaguered capitalism.

It is wrong, however, to see the development of a popular following genuinely committed to an alternative and socialist conception of political values and political possibilities purely as an instrumental political resource for a party (or class) in the quest for power. The relevance of a manipulative perspective is given by the nature of political competition itself; but this

61

perspective is very far from being adequate to register the significance of such competition. Trust can be seen as a manipulated psychic condition, an affective state brought about by the exercise of power from the outside – by the political exponent of capitalist interests or by the leadership of the favoured socialist alternative. But trust can (and must) also be seen as a more or less rational cognitive state, a state of belief at least as much as one of sentiment. As a manipulated psychic condition it might be judged on balance advantageous or disadvantageous to its bearers; but in itself it would simply be a political asset to be disposed of or a political obstacle to be surmounted in the quest for power. As a cognitive state, however, it enjoys a very different form of authority. This is not of course necessarily itself a cognitive authority. Any political judgement is liable to be in error and most political judgements most of the time probably are in crucial respects in error. But the conception of political communities as constituted by agents demands a measure of respect, at the point of political choice, for the cognitive states (however bemused) of all their adult members. As Colonel Rainborough famously put it: '... really I think the poorest he that is in England hath a life to live, as the greatest he; ... and I do think that the poorest man in England is not at all bound in a strict sense to that government that he hath not had a voice to put himself under.'[81] (For 'he' read also 'she' throughout.)

Since in the late twentieth century (as earlier) many men and women find themselves subjected to governments (capitalist and socialist) to which they would not in any sense give their consent and in whose inception they had not the slightest voice, the issue of respect for the constitutional inhibitions of democracy is of pressing urgency for socialist parties. (It is of at least equal importance, for somewhat different reasons, for those parties committed to the defence of capitalist interests.) The suspicion that a socialist party is insincere in its avowals of constitutionalist rectitude is, and should be, acutely politically damaging in the competitive politics of capitalist democracies. This is one of the reasons why any marked discretion over the tyrannical political character of the Soviet government, particularly in relation to Eastern Europe, is now so costly to European communist parties. But it is not merely in such instrumental considerations that the significance of a commitment to democratic procedures lies. Far more important, in fact, is the quite different relation between the presence of popular trust and the existence of a socialist polity, and its presence or absence in a capitalist polity.

No democratic capitalist state rests its claim to legitimacy upon the presumed merits of the capitalist mode of production. Political legitimacy in a capitalist democracy rests simply on the regular presentation to the populace of the opportunity to exercise its own political will. In most democracies most of the time many, if not most, of the population probably feel that the real political options presented to them are less enticing than they would wish. But it is the ideological strength of capitalist democracy to portray the restricted range of options actually presented to the citizenry at large as in the last analysis their own fault. The ideological brunt of capitalist democracy falls not on the contingent (and sometimes exiguous) charms of the political programmes offered by professional politicians but on the equal political right of every citizen to design and present such programmes for themselves. Like any other real state, capitalist democracies in practice depend upon a very extensive political division of labour. But their ideological potency rests finally on the bold but impressive expedient of denying the inevitability of this division of labour and presenting it instead as the sustained choice of every single individual member of the citizen body. This is not ideologically quite as compelling a gesture today as it would have been within the participatory democracy of ancient Athens.[82] It is, however, a great deal more compelling than any alternative which has been offered to it in the last two centuries; and it is incomparably more persuasive than the slyest of apologetic glosses on the political arrangements of all existing, self-proclaimed socialist states. It should not therefore be a matter for much surprise that the combination of liberal democratic constitutional routines with successful capitalist economies should be ideologically highly effective and should be accorded a substantial level of legitimacy by most of the citizenry of countries fortunate enough to enjoy it. But this too is still predominantly an instrumental assessment. It is pragmatically unwise for socialist parties in democratic political competition to give any hint of a desire or disposition to offer less than this in the way of freedom of political choice and expression. What is even more important is that to offer less than this does not merely impair the competitive political appeal of a socialist party, it also blights the grounds on which a socialist claim to political superiority must rest.

Not merely is the purely economic superiority of socialism over capitalism at the productive levels of advanced capitalism eminently contestable and widely contested by economists. It is also no longer today credited at all strongly by any large section of the population of advanced capitalist societies. (There is, as it happens, rather little serious historical analysis of the degree to which and the reasons for which such a purely economic superiority ever has been widely credited anywhere ever.) But if the economic attractions of socialism have markedly diminished for the majority of the inhabitants of advanced capitalist societies (or if, except in the face of immediate sufferings, they have never in fact been especially strong), the cultural revulsion from such societies continues to be relatively intense. It is predominantly to this cultural revulsion that socialist politics has long been a response, and it is on the capacity to give convincing political form to this cultural revulsion – to the sense that these are not a set of terms on which human beings ought to be expected to have to live – that its future prospects mainly depend.

Not merely does a democratic socialist political order require for its practical viability a degree of popular conviction as to its cultural merits: any socialist political order at all depends radically for its pretensions to political superiority over a capitalist state on the force and authenticity of such sentiments. In a capitalist society the legitimacy of the state and the prosperity of the economy are related distantly and contingently. (If this were not so, the legitimacy of the British state except in southern England would long have become threadbare indeed.) Particular candidates for political power, of course, often volunteer more or less intrepidly to take full responsibility for the condition of the economy. But the state itself is not credited automatically with much more than the minimal degree of causal leverage upon the fate of its domestic economy within the world economy at large than it does actually possess. Since international capitalist economics are confessedly anarchic, and since even domestic capitalist production is vividly presented and experienced as largely beyond the reach of intentional control – as an encounter with fatality, not an exercise of will – capitalist democracies enjoy considerable political elasticity in the face of economic decline and misadventure. Individual candidates for political office (and even long-hallowed traditions of political action) can readily lose credibility. But it takes protracted and erratic experience of disaster, and an elaborate concatenation of political contingencies, to subvert the legitimacy of capitalist democracies which have any historical depth.

In contrast, the politics of socialism is inescapably hazardous. As a response to the morally and practically anarchic aspects of capitalist production, socialism is above all else an attempt to reimpose order upon modern social experience through the benign exercise of political authority: to replace the aesthetic, moral and practical anarchy of capitalist production with a new, benign and spiritually compelling order. In the sixteenth and seventeenth centuries in England the struggle to confer moral respectability upon capitalist acts between consenting adults in private was a complex and bitter one, involving a systematic defence of the individual pursuit of personal interest against a residual ideology of communal welfare, and requiring a sustained torture of the existing language of moral approval and disapprobation.[83] But today the defence of the moral propriety of capitalist appropriation and the entitlements which flow from this can afford to be extremely blatant.[84] Socialists by contrast are systematically committed to a certain prudishness over individual desires for material advantage. (No decent person would *keenly* desire to have things.) The distressing historical connections between the claim to establish new social orders which are morally and spiritually superior, the actual practice of tyranny and intolerance, and the systematic inculcation of the most exacting levels of hypocrisy which have often accompanied these, are interpreted in socialist casuistry as regrettable but individually explicable mishaps. There is no reason, of course, why these interpretations should not in each case be wholly valid, and even highly illuminating, as far as they go. But there are certainly aspects of socialist experience which they fall short of explaining. In particular, they fail to register the systematic character of the link between socialism and institutionalized hypocrisy.

Because the political project of socialism is, amongst other goals, to establish a moral and aesthetic order to supplant the moral and aesthetic disorder of capitalism – a cultural remedy for a cultural disfigurement – active popular conviction of its success in having done so is not something with which it can afford to dispense. However, since human beings combine a considerable measure of dispositional scepticism with a marked capacity for social observation, the attempt to generate and sustain such conviction is a labour of Sisyphus. Like colonial rule,[85] socialist politics is a perpetual and necessarily somewhat forlorn struggle to synthesize a degree and style of belief which is simply beyond the credulity of its (passive) targets and which in the end, if taken with too little irony, is likely to prove even beyond the credulity of its active exponents. (The more strenuous the ritual displays of hypocrisy demanded, the more nagging the impulses towards cynicism.)

There are two very different ways of responding to this dilemma: the radical embrace of a cynical instrumentalism, and a more or less shaky recoil into a nervous but dogged ingenuousness. The former plainly has greater intellectual *éclat* and its appeals have been widely ventilated since 1917.[86] As a perspective on politics it perhaps retains the merit of being invigorating. The consequences of its adoption, however, can by now have little appeal for any but the most inveterate scoundrel. A more or less sophisticated ingenuousness, therefore, is likely to prove the last refuge for less disabused socialists. A radically instrumentalist socialist vision sees the main, and as yet unfulfilled, need in socialist politics as the attainment and perpetuation of a higher degree of popular credulity in the merits of socialism. The more ingenuous conception of socialism locates this need instead in the attainment of a higher degree of rational credibility in socialist political organizations and their leaderships. Both instrumental and ingenuous conceptions acknowledge the central importance for socialist politics of the existence of popular trust in socialist political authority and of popular belief in the moral and aesthetic rationality of a socialist order. But the instrumental conception lays the accent firmly on the need for a socialist leadership to secure such trust, and assesses political expedients and strategies, accordingly, in terms of their causal contribution to securing it; while the ingenuous conception lays its stress instead on the need for a socialist leadership to deserve such trust and assesses political expedients and strategies in terms of the causal contribution which they make to the opportunities of the population at large to confer this trust rationally. (Since the tacit preoccupation of political theory is always the exercise of power or the moulding, at least in fantasy, of social and political relations, a focus on the moral responsibilities of those who exercise power is on the whole more reassuring than one which restricts itself solely to the practical opportunities open to those who exercise it.)

XXVI.

No one should mistake the most liberal of capitalist democracies for a political field in which the interests of all citizens compete on fair and equal terms with one another. But the widespread popular conviction within the better-established capitalist democracies that these do represent a more civilized and benign political order than any alternative which has yet been actualized in a modern state is not an ideological mirage. Even as a widespread popular conviction its political importance would be evident enough. But since it happens to be not only widespread but also well-founded, its political importance is difficult to exaggerate.

The internal political pressures to modify capitalist democracies in a socialist direction are certain to continue. They are pressures to modify the capitalist character of their economies and the ugly disfigurements of their social relations which arise from this character. They are certainly not pressures to restrict the very modestly democratic nature of their states. The extent to which such modification is carried through in practice is likely to be principally a function of how far the merits of greater socialization of production are rendered politically convincing, both in the routine competition between political parties for the exercise of governmental power and in broader and more diffuse initiatives in society at large. The cultural revulsion from capitalist organization and its consequences is coeval with these. Whatever may have been true in late-seventeenth-century England, it is quite implausible today to ascribe the political vitality of capitalism to intense conviction of the moral standing of the political entitlements to which it gives rise. Actual appropriation within modern capitalist societies takes place in a more cynical and opportunist, a less elevated, mood. Capitalist institutions are defended, where they are defended, with popular cooperation, as at General Elections, not because they are loved or honoured for themselves but because of the eminently prudent fear that removing them will result in their being replaced with something decidedly worse. This is particularly important in the case of narrowly economic issues. The promise to move an existing capitalist economy in a sharply socialist direction is only likely to prove acceptable, let alone enticing, as a promise (and still more once it begins to be executed, with all the contingent discomforts which will inevitably follow from it), where the electorate is given some serious reason to believe that the transformation can be succcessfully accomplished. A political party which advocates socialist transformation needs, therefore, to be reasonably confident of the practical viability of its intentions and of the prospective benefits of implementing these to at least that portion of the population which it seeks to serve and to lead. But it also needs to extend this confidence as solidly and rationally as it can be extended throughout at least that section of the population. It needs to do so, once again, not merely because otherwise its political followers will not trust it enough to give it power in the first place, but also because these followers will otherwise have too little motive to sustain it in face of the active resistance which any such transformation will definitely meet and of the widespread and often alarming and distressing discomfitures in which it is certain sooner or later to eventuate. (Nothing which could possibly be mistaken for a rapid and irreversible shift in the power and advantages open to private owners of capital has ever failed to elicit active efforts to reverse it.) Popular trust and cultural commitment is as indispensable to a socialist government which presides over ('administers') a fully socialist economy as it is to a socialist party struggling to transform a capitalist economy more or less completely into a socialist economy. In the latter case, clearly, it would be a precondition for the party to muster and hold the political support of the majority in a given political struggle. But in the former case, in any but Elysian circumstances, it will be a necessary condition for a socialist government which permits freedom of political association and expression and real political choice, and which aspires to take, and once it has come into existence cannot any longer avoid taking, full responsibility for the condition of the economy over which it presides, to continue to govern at all. Capitalist government demands only such judicious application of force as the sustaining of the capitalist mode of production from time to time requires. As an institutional structure it has no continuing need for outstanding economic skill or even for the capacity to hold the trust (let alone devotion) of most of its subjects. An uncoercive socialist government requires either a level of intentional control over its economy which there is as yet no reason to believe that human beings are capable of attaining, or a level of trust and commitment from these subjects which it might deserve from the integrity and energy of its efforts, but which it could never hope to earn simply by the splendour of its achievements. It is not just because of the contingencies of the post-war settlement in Eastern Europe or the inherently authoritarian consequences of successful revolutionary struggle that every government in the world today which presides over a reasonably independent and predominantly socialist economy severely restricts freedom of political association and expression and rejects as categorically as it can the possibility of real political choice.

XXVII.

Both the possibility of relatively uncoercive socialist rule and the prospects for further socialization of existing capitalist economies depend therefore in important measure on enhancing the proven efficacy of socialist economic organization. (Socializing economies which have collapsed is not likely in itself to exert a very helpful demonstration effect.) But even if it were literally true that socialist economic organization could never under any circumstances operate more effectively than it has so far succeeded in doing – a presumption which might stretch the credulity even of Professor Hayek – there will continue to be, both in wealthier and in poorer capitalist countries, vigorous if erratic political pressures in a socialist direction. Many of these are certainly pressures in the first instance to redistribute existing stocks of material goods. In this sense they are plainly economic. However, since such pressures are no longer at all cogently linked to a theory of how these stocks of goods can best be augmented in the future, and since the pressures themselves are responses in the first instance to the injustice and ugliness of capitalist relations of production, it is helpful to see them as essentially cultural rather than economic. (As Hume's and Hayek's stress on the utility of the artificial virtues tacitly indicates, the *cultural* authority of the revulsion from capitalism is simply given in human experience and it has to be offset, if it is to be offset at all, by the successful inculcation of ideology or by theoretical demonstration of the superior utility of capitalist production.)

In effect, the natural cultural response to the experience of a capitalist economy is a will to reimpose cultural values upon economic processes: to secure a dominance of the former over the latter (in the earlier stages of capitalist history this was an attempt to reimpose a pre-existing moral economy; more recently it has been the socialist project of subjugating economic process to cultural ideals). One particularly graphic presentation of this response is set out in John Rawls's *Theory of Justice*,[87] which treats the productive capacities of an existing economy and the potential productive powers of the individual members of an existing society as a form of collective asset and assesses the justice of any distribution of the collective product of these members in terms of its contribution to the welfare of the least fortunate among them. A just society, in Rawls's eyes, is very far from being indifferent to economic productivity, since one of its principal commitments is precisely to maximize the economic prosperity of its worst-off members. But, as a society, it subordinates productivity as a value rigorously to the individual and collective good of social justice. Rawls's theory can be interpreted in relation to both socialist and capitalist economic organization, though except on radically implausible theories of economic motivation, it can hardly be seen as compatible with any very rigorous form of economic equality. What it principally implies, for present purposes, is that a morally acceptable society today is one in which culture rules economics. There are many possible grounds for rejecting Rawls's views, some of them resting on explicit moral defence of aspects of capitalist ideology,[88] and others on more intrepidly egalitarian or socialist foundations. At least diagnostically, however, Rawls captures very well the principal form of cultural revulsion from modern capitalist society,[89] and in doing so he makes it evident why this form of revulsion could scarcely cease to be experienced.

Both because of the conditions of political competition in advanced capitalist societies and because of the economic travails of socialism, it is hard for socialist parties in an advanced capitalist society to secure and retain the trust of the majority of its population. Because of the limited success of socialist economic expedients and because of the variety of temptations to which competitors for political power are subject, it is, if anything, even harder for socialist parties to deserve the trust of such a majority. Socialist government is a more extreme and a more hazardous political project than capitalist government – even if exponents of the latter sometimes choose to approach their task in a style which fully matches the highest levels of peril that socialists can threaten. It is so in essence because its presumptive goals are both openly professed and singularly difficult to attain, while capitalist government has no presumptive goals, the character of which is comparably plain; and such goals as it may be thought to be committed to fall most of the time relatively comfortably within its grasp. Capitalist societies in general do require a measure of apathy and expect (and readily admit, at least in peacetime, that they require and expect) relatively low levels of civic virtue in their populace and relatively low levels of political prowess and even honesty on the part of their leaders. But socialist societies, like ancient republics, require relatively high levels of civic virtue in their citizens: like Lord Nelson, they find it hard not to expect that every man, or all but a small criminal element, will do his duty. More alarmingly, they also require high levels of political prowess and equally high levels of honesty on the part of their leaders. Like ancient republics, therefore, socialist societies are, and are likely to remain, distressingly accident-prone. This is why their need for political democracy and for effective institutional guarantees of political liberty is so absolute. Because of the overwhelming conceptual and political pressure upon socialist parties and their leaders to lay claim to the possession of capacities which they necessarily cannot enjoy, and because of the impetus towards self-deception and hypocrisy which issues from this pressure, no socialist party or leader has any right to restrict the struggle to avoid political corruption to the exercise of their own will. The continuing backdrop which democracy offers to the performance of its political protagonists – sceptical, ribald, disabused – is a precondition for the trustworthiness of any socialism: a necessary complement to the politics of its impossibly good intentions.

To secure and deserve the trust of the people (the majority, the working class, if that indeed is the majority) is, other things being equal, the appropriate goal of socialist political action. But the most rhetorically compelling, the most morally rigorous and the most practically skilful of socialist politicians is, in the end, only a politician. The best of socialist parties is, in the end, only a political party. And the best of socialist governments is, in the end, only a government. No politician, no party, and above all no government, however trustworthy and well-intentioned it may be, has any justified political title to protect itself against the possibility that trust will in due course seep away. Socialism without democracy for any length of time (without the rule of law, without the responsibility of governors to governed, without freedom of political expression and association) is too dangerous a political form to deserve the trust of any human beings anywhere. The force of this claim is quite unaffected by the fact that some socialist governments have governed quite well in some respects for reasonably lengthy periods of time. Precisely the same is true of absolute monarchs.

ᴠᴜᴠ

'True Socialism'?

XXVIII.

Few will now be inclined to dispute that the peaceful transition to socialism within capitalist democracies will be at best a hard and obstructed road. But few also, even amongst the more sanguine of revolutionary socialists, would now care to argue in the light of twentieth-century experience that violent revolution, whatever the prospects for its occurrence, is particularly likely to leave in its wake a peaceful, democratic and prosperous socialist society. In politics what is likely to happen is more important than what just conceivably might.

How then, except by the most blatant and strenuous self-deception, does any serious modern observer of politics contrive to remain a socialist? The answer, unsurprisingly, is that the more perceptive and scrupulous of modern socialists remain socialists, increasingly, by dint of confining their intellectual attention more and more firmly to the first two aspects of a political theory (the analysis of existing societies and the theory of social and political goods) at the expense of its third aspect (the analysis of how what exists can be sustained or improved and how social and political goods can in practice be realized). Modern socialism, that is to say, is far from utopian in its negative motivation, in that it bases itself on extensive and sometimes extremely penetrating assessment of capitalist societies as these are. But it is increasingly utopian, not in its stress on the intrinsically desirable, but in its fitful and perfunctory attention to the causal problems of assessing how far this is genuinely realizable even in principle, and how precisely it could in fact be realized in practice. Such contrasts in the intellectual cogency of different components of a political theory is itself unremarkable. It is certainly a less demanding intellectual task to identify defects in an existing set of arrangements and to imagine and describe a set of social and political goods than it is to judge how exactly to realize these goods through political action. (An obvious example of the comparative robustness in its grasp of existing defects and malfunctions in capitalist economies, as compared with the hazy and fantastical character of its conceptions of how and at what cost these defects and malfunctions might be remedied, would be the conservative monetarist response to the inflationary crisis of the late 1970s.)

It simply is harder for any human beings, conservatives and liberals just as much as socialists, to judge what to do than it is to identify what is at present amiss or what should ideally be preferred. Conservatives make this disparity the fulcrum of an entire political theory and, with more intermittent success if less questionable sincerity, they seek to ground their practical political activities as firmly as they can upon its implications. (If it is hard to achieve intended effects, unambitious intentions, other things being equal, can expect a less discouraging outcome than ambitious intentions.) The more ambitious and practically directed forms of liberalism[90] balance their recognition of the difficulty of achieving intended effects by adopting a restricted range of second-order intentions, putting their trust in such mechanisms as the 'invisible hand' of the market, which supposedly yield a desired social outcome which could not be dependably secured by direct attempts to promote it. For liberals the principal merit of a capitalist society is the centrality to it of such invisible hand mechanisms. Both conservatives and liberals, despite their explicit regard for the political importance of prudence, find it in practice (like anyone else) difficult politically to realize their desires. Each of them in modern capitalist democracies acts primarily defensively and within the framework of a society already firmly in existence. Since what socialists aspire to do is to alter these societies very extensively indeed, their need for prudence and realism is far more acute than that of their opponents – for whom, for much of the time, simple inertia will furnish much of such prudence as they require. This need is not just morally more acute (in that more ambitious intentions, other things being equal, can expect a more discouraging outcome: a hazard that can be offset, if at all, only by superior causal judgement); it is also politically more acute, even in the first instance. To obtain the opportunity to govern at all, socialists who do overtly intend to transform an existing society must appear *capable* of transforming it very broadly as they intend. They must appear practically effective and do so in the teeth of the derisive commentary of their political opponents. Because their causal ambitions are greater than those of their opponents (in the deliberate moulding of social relations, if not in the competition to secure political power), their need to be effective is correspondingly greater also. From a wholly instrumental and short-term viewpoint, to be sure, the semblance of greater efficacy will suffice on its own to give them a chance to win power. But even from a purely instrumental point of view it will hardly suffice for very long, since the popular response to ineffective socialist transformation is seldom enthusiastic, and since it is at least as easy to reverse progress towards socialism within a reasonably liberal capitalist democracy as it is to make the progress in the first place. The need for a convincing account of what to do in order to realize socialist values, in this perspective, is just another facet of the discouraging political experience of democratic socialism.

XXIX.

There is, however, another way of thinking about socialism: a way which refuses in the first instance to consider the nagging perplexities of practical choice and focuses instead on the question of what in human social relations truly deserves allegiance, admiration and even love. Actually existing socialism, either in its full-blown (or slowly deflating) Soviet or Chinese incarnations or in its decidedly more stunted western avatars in Sweden or France or even, residually, the United Kingdom, is a sorry enough affair with little claim, either moral or aesthetic, on human enthusiasm or commitment. (It may nevertheless be superior to any practical alternative.) But True Socialism would be, or perhaps will be, quite different. True Socialism is, by definition, the full realization of the socialist conception of the good. It has not as yet, except very fleetingly and on a small number of occasions, been seen in operation on the face of the earth. But its time will, or might, or could come; perhaps even come about everywhere and for the rest of human time. (Something of this kind appears to be what Marx was promising in the *German Ideology* and the *Communist Manifesto*, though it is possible that he did not in fact fully believe it himself and it certainly sits very oddly with the brutally sceptical realism of most of his vision of human societies as they were at the time and had developed in the past.) It is not easy to interpret the subjunctives and counterfactuals, or even perhaps the simple future tenses, in such claims. But what underlies them is the judgement, seldom made very explicit, that it is possible and legitimate to think about social and political possibility through the prism of the intrinsically desirable rather than by assessing existing societies and judging how exactly these can in practice be changed. This judgement is hardly one open to anyone who subscribes without reservations to Marx's own theory of history – or at least it is hardly one which could be adopted by such a subscriber without grotesque intellectual confusion. But it has deep roots in the tradition of utopian moralizing; and within its own, in the last resort, somewhat apolitical, terms, it can be coherent enough.

XXX.

Because True Socialism is a utopian construction, it is not doomed to evasion or mendacity over, or to complicity in, existing social and political distortions, as any equation of an existing society with True Socialism is bound to be. True Socialism as a mode of utopian thought is, or at least would like to see itself as being, open to any of the political lessons which historical experience has thus far provided. But it refuses to be restricted within the narrow imaginative confines of men's past historical achievements. True Socialism is socialism undistorted by the obstructive effects of existing social and political power and perhaps unblemished by the malign impact of this power upon men's political imaginations. (The optimism of this last expectation is evident enough.) It has been widely remarked that experience of the increasing complexity of advanced industrial societies, amongst other pressures, has had a blighting effect over the last few decades upon utopian thinking, in large measure supplanting this with pronouncedly dystopian reflections. On the whole this effect has been at least as marked in the case of socialism as it has with any other modern tendency in political theory. In consequence the impetus towards socialism, already damagingly utopian in its neglect of issues of practical efficacy, has become increasingly feeble even in its imaginative aspirations. True, it has somewhat extended the range of these aspirations, acknowledging the superficiality (and even malignity) of its previous understanding of women's opportunities, needs and rights, of the ecological costs of modern industrial and agricultural production and of the problematic relation between industrial and non-industrial countries. But it has done so in a superficial and disaggregated manner, in an undignified scurry to increase the constituency of its potential supporters and to ward off particularly painful forms of moral vituperation. Partly because of this (in itself predominantly praiseworthy) accommodation, the socialist conception of the good has become increasingly miscellaneous and weakly integrated, leaving the more utopian forms of socialist sentiment — those unwilling to rest contented with a very modest social democracy like the Britain of the late 1960s, or with the authoritarian socialism of the Soviet Union — increasingly bereft of any clear conception of utopia, of just what it is that they have good reason politically to desire and value. Because of the unsystematic and disjointed manner in which it has been compiled, the socialist conception of the good has become little more than a series of extensions of the socialist critique of capitalist society, a critique which is probably richer in causal understanding today than it has ever been before, but which, because it is founded solely on a distaste for existing experience, is not necessarily politically any more wisely directive than Blanqui's celebrated proclamation: 'What exists is bad. Something else must take its place.'[91] Since in advanced capitalist societies any literate person has ample opportunity to discover that much of the globe displays conditions which are strikingly nastier than what at present exists within their own communities, a political programme founded on nothing but an accumulation of local aversions is far from compelling.

It is not at present clear whether it is actually possible to identify and articulate a coherent socialist conception of what is politically good or desirable. Nor is there any definite reason at present to believe that such a conception must necessarily be any less clear, coherent and compelling than, for example, a liberal conception of the good.[92] Without some progress in specifying this conception, it is difficult to see how socialists can expect either to muster much dependable popular commitment to altering society in a socialist direction, or to sustain any great assurance of their own over just what forms of social modification genuinely are examples of socialist development. It is reasonable to hope that True Socialism would be very different, and different in predominantly attractive ways, from the contemporary Soviet Union or modern Sweden. But any such hope is only politically relevant if True Socialism means something decidedly more robust than the set of all politically or socially attractive characteristics of which a particular political theorist happens to be able to think. Here the issue of the symmetry or asymmetry of political judgement is crucial. True Socialism differs from the real world by definition. But if it is to play a benign role in guiding political judgement and in orientating political action it must differ from the real world in cognitively more taxing ways than simple individual assertion. In particular, it is indispensable for a socialist conception of political and social good to be grounded just as firmly in considered causal judgements as is the socialist critique of existing capitalist societies. If the asymmetry between True Socialism and socialist expedients which happen to have been tested in practice is claimed to be too great, this has two major consequences. The first is to turn True Socialism into a political and social condition in the possible actualization of which no one can have very good reason to believe. The second is to provide formidable weapons of ideological self-defence in the face of the discouragements of experience. It is clear enough that the second consequence plays an important role in motivating the insistence on the drastic asymmetry between True Socialism and such socialist institutions or societies as happen thus far to have come into existence. Hence the massive scholasticism of discussions of socialist conceptions of the good, their heavy grounding in scriptural citation and their infuriating tendency towards a purely verbal circularity. For those socialists who already hold state power, ideological self-defence in the face of the discouragements of experience does offer, at least for a limited time, a combination of psychic relief with the opportunity to continue to exercise power. But for socialists who do not as yet exercise state power such psychic ease as it affords is likely to be purchased at some little political cost. The political question for socialists is always, in part, one of how many men and women can be induced to suspend their disbelief in the merits of a socialist organization of some or all aspects of society. Ideological self-defence is a weak persuasive tactic.

XXXI.

A bolder and politically more promising approach is to ask plainly and frankly whether or not there is good reason to expect any actual socialist institution or society to realize a socialist conception of political good: to consider directly the question of whether this conception itself is in fact causally coherent. Most elaborated social and political ideals are of somewhat dubious causal coherence — products of what Goethe ungenerously titled 'the beautiful dream-wish of mankind'.[93] It would be surprising if socialist ideals were altogether exempt from this defect. Since socialism aspires to synthesize, with extraordinary ambition, a passionate and compulsive revulsion from a particular concrete social experience with the enactment of an extremely exigent set of social and political values, the grounds for doubting its causal coherence are especially acute.

Would even the Truest Socialism really represent a marked improvement on the very patchily socialized advanced capitalist economies and societies of countries like Britain or Sweden? Socialists who respond to this question merely with firm expressions of faith need not be compromising their own sincerity: sincerity is a rigorously subjective condition. But they will hardly be giving impressive evidence of their political intelligence; and they will be refusing even to attempt to give reasons to anyone else for sharing their own faith. To extend this conviction on a rational basis to very many others, which both evaluatively and causally would be a necessary condition for realizing True Socialism, requires the provision of cogent reasons. Such reasons for particular human beings can only in principle be located within their own existing apparatus of beliefs about society or within modifications of this apparatus which experience, including the experience of political reasoning, leads them to make. Any credible, and therefore politically effective, version of True Socialism must be rendered credible through its congruence with the perceptions of what human beings are like and of why institutions work or fail to work as they do, which its auditors already possess. To insist on any very sharp asymmetry between True Socialism and the lessons of historical experience is therefore not merely a form of imaginative self-indulgence for socialist thinkers; it is also an explicit repudiation of the sole means through which socialist belief can extend itself in a democratic and rational fashion. A public and rationally assessable interpretation of True Socialism, as opposed to a private and fideist conception, can only be grounded in the assumption of a very large degree of symmetry between existing experience and social or political potential. (This does not in itself tell us how much better True Socialism might actually prove; it merely tells us how to think about the question of how much better True Socialism might actually prove.)

Fideist versions of True Socialism proclaim confidently that within it all manner of things shall be well. Men and women under True Socialism will be quite different from the way they are now: noble, virtuous, disciplined, generous, dedicated, indefatigable, selfless, rational, patient, gentle, resolute, courageous, friendly, independent, cooperative, adaptable, discerning, cheerful, perhaps even artistic. They will assuredly not be cowardly, lazy, mean, malicious, rigid, competitive, envious, selfish, morose, obtuse, nervous, cruel, cynical, improperly sceptical, hypocritical, hard-hearted or mutually suspicious. Any society in which all or most of its members did indeed exhibit the sterling qualities promised would certainly be a marked improvement on a society, otherwise identical, in which they regrettably did not. A society in which all or most of its members felt less anxious, harassed and neglected than they do under advanced capitalism and in which all or most enjoyed themselves more than they at present have the opportunity to do, would foster *some* of the nicer qualities in these lists and diminish the stimuli to some of the nastier. But the idea that human performance in any society might simply consist of instances of the relevant virtues without a trace of the relevant vices could hardly be a rational inference from anyone's experience; and the view that it could be caused to come to consist only of such instances through the deft exercise of political authority ought to strain anyone's credulity. If True Socialism were actually to work more agreeably and reassuringly than existing forms of society, capitalist or socialist, it would be reasonable to expect this superiority to exercise a benign influence on the dispositions of its members, particularly if it proved to persist through several successive generations. What is emphatically not reasonable is to anticipate that True Socialism would in practice work more agreeably and reassuringly than existing forms of society *because* within it – by stipulation – men and women would dependably exhibit all the canonical socialist virtues. Such a claim is not merely politically undirective; it has no rational bearing whatever on political choice or judgement. And since it manifestly does exert some influence on political nerve and emotion, it is, for all its apparent tautologousness, blatantly deceptive.

To construct a socialist conception of the good which does have some real, because deserved, bearing upon political choice, it is necessary to consider Truly Socialist institutions or a Truly Socialist society from a causal point of view, asking how exactly they should be expected to operate and why they should be expected to operate in that way rather than in some other.

To do this, even perfunctorily, it is helpful to separate in the first place the political from the economic attributes of a genuinely socialist society – not, of course, because these are causally independent of one another but because, although causally inseparable, they are nevertheless analytically distinct and problematic in very different ways. The essence of True Socialism[94] is the presumption that culture can rule, that economic and political structures can be transposed into purely social relations, undistorted by arbitrary coercion or conflict of real interests. This presumption was derived by the young Marx from an extremely grandiose and hazardous (if undeniably exciting) style of thinking. Subsequent historical experience has done nothing to confirm the judiciousness of this presumption. But it does, perhaps, bear rather tangentially on its validity. (What this experience shows, perhaps, is not what True Socialism is really like but merely that True Socialism has no bearing whatever on real political possibilities.) The view that True Socialism will be a relatively effortless product of the immanent development of capitalist society, or even that it is at all likely to appear in particular countries simply as the result of a domestic political débâcle on the part of capitalist interests has lost whatever rational plausibility it may ever have possessed. Indeed, the conditions in which socialism has actually made its way through history, in society after society, were in virtually every instance glaringly unpropitious for the emergence of True Socialism. The most vivid and urgent suspicion about socialism, sharply reinforced by experience of some of the least propitious of these episodes – the Great Purge, Kampuchea under Pol Pot[95] – is that it may both require for its survival, and guarantee by its survival, a considerably more authoritarian style of rule than that to which inhabitants of capitalist democracies have become accustomed. In the historical course of socialist thinking, there have been versions of True Socialism which have frankly acknowledged (and even gloried in) this requirement. But the great bulk of socialist thinking has been understandably eager to repudiate any permanent need of this kind for systematic repression and has sought instead to portray True Socialism, at least after its initial teething troubles (the dictatorship of the proletariat, primitive accumulation etc.), as a particularly uncoercive social regimen. The fact that there have been remarkably barbarous forms of socialist tyranny (and that there remain moderately barbarous forms of the same) no more proves that socialism has to be tyrannical than the fact that there have been at least equally barbarous forms of capitalist tyranny (and that here too there remain in some quantity moderately barbarous forms of the same) demonstrates that capitalism ensures tyranny. What is quite clear is that both capitalism and socialism *permit* tyranny. To preserve either a socialist or a capitalist productive system in particular countries at particular times can require a very high level of arbitrary violence; and the destructive legacy of such violence, in either case, can last for decades.

Any serious account of the purely political properties of True Socialism must rest, therefore, on a direct consideration of the process through which True Socialism is to be inaugurated and not elect to evade this issue by invoking the inscrutability of the future. (If the future really were comprehensively inscrutable, none of us could have any rational basis at all for our political opinions and judgements.) In practice, therefore, the account must largely retrace the lines of argument which we have already considered in chapter 2, seeking to assess the potential for a peaceful and democratic transition to socialism within capitalist democracies, for a non-authoritarian outcome of violent revolutionary transformations of these societies and for a peaceful or violent internal transformation of the existing authoritarian socialist regimes which have emerged or which will emerge in the future from violent revolution. It is essential to face this question, because avoiding it obviates the possibility of assessing the practical relevance of True Socialism. For if the latter is simply historically inaccessible, if it amounts only to a more or less coherent set of social ideals which cannot be realized by any possible sequence of historical action, its capacity to guide and illuminate political action will depend abjectly on men's ability to recognize this inaccessibility and draw the rigorous conclusions which follow from it. To have high standards is splendid in itself; but to expect to realize these standards in the face of the refractoriness of others (and hence at their expense) can only be defensible if these standards could in principle be realized. A combination of high standards (and the self-righteousness which accompanies the consciousness of possessing these) with systematically over-optimistic practical judgement[96] is a proven recipe for political disaster and a fundamentally corrupt form of political consciousness. It is not an accident that highly moralistic and unrealistic self-righteousness of this kind should have repeatedly mutated, under conditions of real political action, into an essentially nihilist machiavellianism. True Socialism is conceived, by some, as the inscription of desired values upon blank paper: as *carte blanche* socialism. As an artificial device for conceptual analysis, this might in principle be perfectly coherent.[97] But as a basis for political judgement, it could hardly be less appropriate. If *carte blanche* socialism is not simply an intellectual conceit but rather a political project which men and women may seek deliberately to implement, the blank sheets of paper will consist of the bodies and minds of human beings. An unpleasant but revealing example of a real attempt to implement *carte blanche* socialism has been provided by the Kampuchean experiment under Pol Pot. True Socialism is an intellectual's, or a political entrepreneur's, conception of how the rest of the human race ought to, and perhaps could be induced to, live their lives. It may be culturally egalitarian in its estimate of human merits; but because it is a proposal from intellectuals and political entrepreneurs who are confident of knowing better, to common men and women who are implicitly proclaimed to know worse (if indeed at all), it is politically very inegalitarian indeed. Because men's or women's understanding of politics does vary immensely in depth and precision, this political inegalitarianism is not necessarily just an impertinence. But it does demand a recognition, and an attempt to shoulder, massive cognitive responsibilities. *Carte blanche* socialism, with only the most cognitively frivolous or morally disingenuous conception of how the transition to this is to be implemented, may in the nineteenth century have been a purely intellectual misdemeanour. But given the fearsome repressive energies of modern state powers (the torture chambers, the labour camps and the mass graves), it has become by the late twentieth century a major political menace.

XXXII.

Under True Socialism (conceived merely as an analytical device) how should we imagine the exercise of political power? Under True Socialism, more crassly, who is going to tell whom to do what? And why are those whom they tell going to act, or refuse to act, as instructed? And how is the pattern of their compliance or dissidence going to come out for the better? On the great chess board of human society, as Adam Smith helpfully pointed out, every single piece has a principle of motion of its own.[98] How are they to move benignly in concert? Under True Socialism (as with any other set of human political and social arrangements) very many human beings will be doing very many different things. How and why will these myriad activities harmonize for the better? One interpretation of True Socialism resolutely rejects the role of political choice and authority in securing these happy results. Under True Socialism no one will possess or will need to possess the authority to tell anyone to do anything. This is a pleasant fantasy; but as a thesis about political possibilities it is a transparent confession of bad faith. For how exactly, if no one is going to tell anyone to do (or not to do) anything, are the autonomous and independent performances of the entire citizenry (most of them at least as practically ingenious and as quirky in their tastes as you or me) to be coordinated? And why should their collective consequences come out for the better? Under True Socialism, on an optimistic construction, political authority might become less arbitrary in its control over, and more directly responsible to, the citizen body, in localities and productive units, in entire industries and even nationally. (Since most production is now in some measure integrated and rationalized trans-nationally, even this herculean achievement would give any particular populace rather limited collective control of much of their destiny.) Men and women might be better educated, less deceived, less anxious and more public-spirited. They might agree more on how their society should be organized and they might prove more responsive to their own personal standards of justice and duty than they have sufficient motive and energy to be today. However, since they would retain minds of their own they might also, of course, agree even less on how their society should be organized and, while desiring more keenly and seeking more energetically to live virtuously, differ every bit as sharply as they do at present on just what forms of action virtue in fact requires of them. But since they would continue to see the world for themselves and to find themselves in markedly diverse practical situations, and since all of them would continue to be extremely imperfectly informed about the situations of most other human beings, they will certainly continue to require institutions for taking political decisions and for ensuring adherence to these decisions once they have been taken.

Because socialism aspires to subordinate the workings of all human institutions to benign cultural values, instead of abandoning most of the responsibility for the workings of production to the supposedly automatic operations of the market, it is compelled to trust more expansively to the effectiveness and benignity of its political institutions than most capitalist societies most of the time have occasion to do. (The only capitalist societies which acknowledge a comparable need are those that find themselves forced to submit to one or other variety of dictatorial rule to preserve a predominantly capitalist economy from threats of further socialization.) This certainly implies that socialist politics has a more urgent need than it normally cares to recognize to imbibe the lessons of the political tradition of power-diffusing institutional design which go back to the European Ancien Regime: the emphasis on constitutionalism, the rule of laws rather than men and the mechanisms for ensuring governmental accountability which were explored in the writings of Montesquieu, Hume, Madison or de Tocqueville. The source of socialist confidence that political coordination of men's activities on a large scale can readily be unproblematic lies in a distinctive and intensely moralistic style of political vision which identifies as the sole source of political hazard – once the corrupt institutions of aristocracy or capitalism have been at last displaced – the slyness and moral undependability (the egoism) of mankind. It is a political style memorably exemplified by the Parisian *sans-culottes* in the fervently demotic rituals of their Sectional assemblies, and best epitomized in the condemnation of Citoyen Bourdon of the Section de Bonne-Nouvelle in the year II[99] for voting in a low voice. The view that human slyness and moral undependability are politically important, however archaic in expression, is a judgement which has·withstood the test of historical experience rather well, though the view that it is a hazard which can be dealt with effectively by sustaining a high level of public moral excitement has definitely worn less well. But there are many other impediments to social transparency and political agreement than a human propensity to be less than perfectly frank. Indeed the idea that a continuous display of perfect frankness by all human beings all the time would make for an amicable, reassuring and conflict-free society does no justice at all to the portentous degree to which civilized human social relations rest upon the (often unavailing)[100] struggle to display discretion and tact: to conceal the frequently trivial but nonetheless keen embarrassment, revulsion and even horror, or the helpless mirth with which men and women are apt to regard each other.

There are at present two principal types of mechanism for coordinating human activity within a particular territorial society, one of which also works quite effectively to coordinate human activities between territorial societies. The first of these is institutionalized political authority. Coordination by command is compatible with quite high levels of practical citizen participation, freedom of expression and freedom of inquiry, as well, of course, as with exceedingly low levels of any of these. The political aspects of True Socialism, it seems fair to say, have on the whole been envisaged both vaguely and evasively. But they could certainly be considered more precisely and honestly without much difficulty. If so considered, they would be unlikely to appear transcendently more attractive in themselves than the politics of capitalist democracies, but it ought at least to be possible to be confident whether or not they need to be overwhelmingly less attractive than these. At present it is still reasonable to hope that they could be rendered (and kept) somewhat more attractive to most than the politics of capitalist democracies are ever likely to become.

The second principal mechanism for coordinating human activities today is the system of market exchange which is central to capitalist production. Socialists in general and Marxists in particular are for the most part extremely hostile to the market, seeing its operations as offensively untransparent, anarchic and wasteful. In place of the amoral disorder of the market, they offer as a clearly superior alternative determinant of what human beings are to produce and how they are to do so, a single directing rational will of the society as a whole (and perhaps in the end of the existing adult population of the world as a whole). Societies as wholes, of course, and still more the entire adult world population at any time, do not actually possess a directing rational will of their own, though in the world today they will certainly possess a government which is eager to present itself in this guise. In existing socialist economies, accordingly, the invisible hand of the market is largely replaced as coordinator of production by the often all too visible fist of the state. It is probable that some of the politically repressive qualities of existing socialist states do not assist the effective coordination of production. But what the experience of these states does make clear is that subjecting an entire economy to a single rational will is a difficult, and may be even an impossible, task. The politics of True Socialism may have been described evasively; but the economics of True Socialism are at present closer to an exercise in pure magic. Considered from a safe distance and in firm detachment from the vicissitudes of particular participants, the market is an effective coordinator of interests because it relies for its working on simple and robust, if not especially enticing, aspects of human motivation. But the design of an economy coordinated by command must either rely for most of its workings on precisely the same aspects of human motivation (material incentives) or on the use of expedients (moral incentives) which may sound more edifying but which in application prove not merely less dependable but decidedly uglier. (Moral incentives misliked are simply blackmail at the receiving end.) It is reasonable to cast doubt on the relevance of the political methods of existing socialist states to the politics of True Socialism, if less reasonable to regard the latter with unfettered optimism without troubling to think systematically about their working or to explain how they are to be inaugurated. But it is wholly unreasonable to ignore the relevance of the economic experience of existing socialist states to the economics of True Socialism. Not only is there every reason to believe that the governments of these states would hasten to adopt effective techniques of economic organization if these were clearly and readily available, there is also some reason to believe that, throughout their history, many of their more egregious political features have been a direct product of the intellectual and practical difficulties of organizing a socialist economy.[101] (Some of their marked reluctance to adopt fresh organizational expedients, of course, is simply a consequence of the sinister interest of existing holders of power at many levels. But to presume that the structure of sinister interests in any society is solid and integrated enough at the level of its state power to forestall indefinitely obvious and major productive improvements is to underestimate both the plasticity and capacity for initiative of political power and the rich political rewards of successful innovation.)

The record of socialist economic planning has not been in any sense uniformly disastrous. In the last half century, for example, it has turned the Soviet Union into the second most powerful military power on earth and, in a limited number of settings for a period of time, it has achieved rates of economic growth as rapid as, and steadier than, most of the capitalist world. Planning techniques have gained greatly in sophistication and technical intricacy; and understanding of the causal properties of socialist economies has also grown impressively (both inside and outside socialist countries).[102] In some respects socialist economies compare extremely well with capitalist economies at roughly similar levels of wealth, particularly from the viewpoint of the industrial manual work force: far better security of employment, less oppressive work rates, even, in some cases, steadier economic growth. Systematic comparisons between the records of capitalist and socialist economies are technically very difficult to carry out for a variety of reasons. But on present showing they do not establish a clear general superiority in economic efficiency either of socialist over capitalist production or vice versa. On the whole, however, it would be fair to say that the experience of socialist economic planning, particularly in relatively advanced and highly industrialized economies, has been at best mildly discouraging. If it has not fully confirmed the arguments of Hayek and von Mises that socialist economic planning is utterly impracticable, it has identified a considerable range of intractable, and perhaps insurmountable, impediments to its working at all high levels of efficiency. Most importantly of all, it has made intellectually indefensible the image of integral rational control as a real alternative to the causal determination of economic outcomes through (no doubt highly distorted) market mechanisms. Socialist economic planning certainly is a real alternative to a market economy; but it equally certainly is not in reality a form of integral rational control. Indeed it is not even clear that socialist planning offers effective remedies for some of the most obvious defects of market exchange: notably the incapacity of markets to assess and take account of the external costs and gains of particular transactions or production decisions. The record of socialist economies in encouraging technical innovation and entrepreneurial functions, such as risk-bearing and organizational inventiveness, does show patches of success. But except in areas of massive political concentration such as military research and development, the most careful academic studies suggest, and Russian economists and managers implicitly confirm, that no existing socialist economic institutions can match the prowess of multinational capitalist corporations.[103] Socialist plans limp along behind actual productive processes, becoming out of date as soon as they cease to be pure projections of the future and come to be employed in the contemporary management of the economy. Thus far the experience of socialist planning provides no reason whatever for supposing that it is possible even in principle to gather and respond to the volume of accurate economic information which would be required to render socialist production orderly and free from gross waste (and hence evidently superior to capitalist production in the terms in which socialists have long – and cogently – criticized the latter). It is now generally acknowledged that the record of socialist agriculture has been discouraging in virtually every instance and that only a considerable measure of more or less overt reversion to private production for a market, from China to Hungary, has prevented it from being close to calamitous. It has become evident, too, that socialist economies display an extremely limited interest in the needs and tastes of the actual consumers of the goods which they produce, and that it is difficult in principle to reorganize them to be at all responsive to such needs. Some of these irrationalities and inefficiencies are a product of the highly distorted incentive structures which result from existing ways of organizing socialist production in Russia or China or Poland. Many of these distortions have long been recognized in the ruling circles of socialist states and continue to be maintained largely because of the effective powers of obstruction of those who benefit directly from them or have simply learnt painfully to live with them. There are at least three sharply differentiated organizational formats for the operation of a socialist economy, on display at present in the Soviet Union, Hungary and Yugoslavia, each of which possesses its own merits and disabilities. There are also naturally a considerable range of proposed economic reforms, most suggesting a sharp extension of market relations and, amongst those whose exponents come from outside existing ruling circles, a major diminution in the degree of economic power and initiative concentrated at the centre of these states. It would be absurd, of course, to contrast the workings of any actual socialist economy with a presumptively perfect market system without attendant social costs, or to reject socialist economic planning on the grounds that the consumption opportunities of the great majority of the Russian population fall short of those available to the great majority of the American or Swiss populations. But it is both absurd and dishonest to claim that a conception of True Socialism as the realization of socialist economic, political and social ideals has any relevance at all to rational political choice and action, without bothering to explain how exactly the economy of True Socialism should be presumed to operate.[104]

The historical experience of socialist economic planning does not establish that capitalist production is unequivocally superior, in its capacity to produce for human needs and tastes, to any possible form of socialist production. It does abundantly establish, however, that from the point of view of human flourishing socialist production is just as intricately and refractorily problematic as capitalist production. Some of its commoner defects are rather different from those common in its capitalist rival, though some (such as its propensity fecklessly to pollute and deface human habitats) have proved to be distressingly similar. If True Socialism is to be a coherent representation of a benign polity, society and economy (and not a mere exercise in self-sedating wish-fulfilment) it must embody a representation of an economic system which there is good reason to believe would work effectively in practice. On present evidence, we have good reason to believe that the contrast between capitalist disorder and injustice and the order and justice of True Socialism is too sharply drawn to be intellectually defensible and that its utilization in political dispute as a picture of what a society could be like (and not simply as an expression of what we might ideally desire) is profoundly disingenuous. It would no doubt be unwise to expect even the truest of socialist societies to be populated solely by saints of keen practical intelligence; but even if such a society were populated solely by saints, it would still require a real economy; and the successful organization of that economy would require an extraordinarily high level of intellectual and practical skill, a level immensely higher than human beings have ever yet attained in concerted social and political action, and quite possibly higher than human intelligence and capacity to cooperate in fact permit. Given the indispensability and difficulty of developing such skill in coordination, there is very little reason to regard the circumstances of *carte blanche* socialism as significantly more propitious for the extension of effectively socialist institutions and policies than a capitalist democracy with a reasonably confident and self-organized industrial working class, a strong socialist political movement and a capable socialist intelligentsia. The careful comparison between particular socialist expedients and the particular capitalist alternatives at present in operation in individual societies is the only politically appropriate way to extend socialism, except in conditions of social and political collapse. Where 'True Socialism' is deployed to question the integrity and moral seriousness of such an approach, and not to assist in clarifying the merits and defects of particular lines of policy, what it offers in its stead is nothing but a mirage.

XXXIII.

The hope that culture may prove able to rule economic and political structure, that the shape and texture of social relations might come in their entirety to be determined by, and thus to express, explicit and conscious human values has had some ideological resonance in most reasonably successful human societies. It is an imaginatively natural and evocative way of rendering the determination to take these values seriously. But within actual fields of political and social conflict and in the face of the Machiavellian importunities and expedients of political agency, it is not a wholly benign way of expressing this determination. One defect of it has been well captured by Robert Nozick in his critique of Rawls.[105] Nozick's own political theory is neither illuminating nor edifying; but some of his criticisms of liberal and socialist conceptions of social justice cut extremely deep. The socialist need to prohibit some capitalist acts between consenting adults, to set some restrictions on the right to give and to tax the citizenry, are hardly occasions for acute alarm (though the lengths to which some socialist states have felt it necessary to go in attempting to stamp out capitalist acts between consenting adults have scarcely been well considered either morally or practically).[106] But the relation between what Nozick calls 'pattern theories' of justice and the imaginative basis of certain types of socialist authority claims is a genuinely close one.[107] Historical production has taken place outside a moralized history (in pre-socialist time). It now offers a set of resources which are available for reallocation by political authority (how else?) in order to realize the values of socialism: to make history at last moral and society at last just. As a politically inert moral theory, there is no reason why this should not be intellectually coherent and morally cogent. But as a practical political theory it is rather more hazardous. In politics it is governments who must identify the moral patterns and cause them to be realized in practice. Although the material resources produced by past human action are at any time wholly open to reallocation to realize such patterns, this reallocation is not a once-and-for-all performance but a continuous task. What makes it endless is the continuing tendency of the history of human action to disrupt the pattern. Because the pattern (social ideals) deserves to rule, history (the actions of most members of society) is a perpetual display of (at best inadvertent) moral insubordination. Governments, *just* governments, as the dutiful and obedient instruments of the pattern, sustain moral order against this incessant dissidence. The history of (just) government is a history of moral commitment. Individual private citizens, of course, may have the highest moral qualities; and all private citizens might choose to observe their legal duties punctiliously; but the history of the actions of the citizenry as a whole is not a moral history, since considered severally in their entirety the citizens do not have a moral role. (None of this sounds very like the education of the educators.)

This is not, of course, a criticism of the theory of Rawls himself, which is both politically vaguer and more democratic. Still less is it an endorsement of the moral standing of American political and economic institutions or those of any other capitalist country. But it does serve as a helpful reminder that it is wise to inspect with some care the suggestion that the disorderly and teasing substance of any real society can be brought briskly into line with the demands of our moral intuitions.

If so, exactly how?

ʊɯ

Moral

XXXIV.

True Socialism is the socialist conception of the good or intrinsically desirable society unimpeded in its practical realization by social, political or economic causality. It is to be preferred to all forms of socialism or capitalism which exist or have existed, as the pure objects of desire are to be preferred to the possibly attainable goals of action. It cannot tell human beings what they have good reason to do. But what it does offer is rather firm guidance on some forms of political agency which socialists have good reason to avoid. (Political theory in general cannot tell human beings what to do. What it can tell them is what not to forget.)

The idea that human social, economic and political relations can be brought perfectly into conformity with our moral intuitions and kept in such conformity more or less indefinitely is excessively optimistic as a practical expectation. (The view that this will come about quasi-automatically in practice sooner or later, with the aid of a little timely violence, is simply deranged.) But the idea that human beings are likely to continue to desire their social, economic and political relations to express their moral intuitions and to attempt, other things being equal, to cause them to do so is sober and realistic enough. These intuitions, to be sure, arise out of experience of and reflection upon such relations, amidst an endless political and social struggle to define the terms in which this experience is best captured. In any large-scale society at any one time they are never very homogeneous; and there is no reason whatsoever to believe that they would become particularly homogeneous, even if purged of all the false factual beliefs and errors of logic which they happen at present to contain. Like any extended passage of human history, the history of socialism has been in many ways a disappointing one, while the history of capitalism, by contrast, has up to now been far less disappointing than Marx in the later 1840s expected it to prove. Yet there remain within all capitalist societies, and perhaps inseparable from capitalist production and exchange itself (from the system of ownership on which it depends), forms of inhumanity and injustice which violate the moral sensibilities of most of their inhabitants with some historical consistency. The political form which the responses to this sense of violation assume has varied very greatly from society to society and there is every reason to expect it to continue to do so. It is determined by the political understanding and skill of leaders, in dialogue with the imaginations of a population at large, and by the chance contingencies of geopolitics as well as by the economic histories of the countries concerned. In some cases (such as the United States) socialism has played a very minor role in its political expression and virtually no role at all in bringing it to bear upon the exercise of governmental power.[108] In other instances, where the political and cultural tide towards socialism has flowed strongly for many decades, this tide may well ebb dramatically for a time through the political maladroitness of its exponents, the skill and luck of its foes, the internal contradictions of the particular forms of action in which it has been brought politically to bear, or the distrust and despondency of its traditional supporters. But there is no realistic possibility of this tide simply petering out. The economic and political mechanisms which created the relative tranquillity of advanced capitalist societies in the early and mid-1960s, the era of Lipset, Shonfield and the end of ideology,[109] were in large measure political products of this cultural distaste for capitalist production. The politics of the last decade in advanced, as in less advanced, capitalist countries has been devoted largely to the reversal of these social-democratic mitigations of capitalist disfigurements, because of the severe restraints which they had come to impose upon the profitability of capitalist enterprise as a whole. From a socialist point of view this may have appeared simply the history of a sequence of bewildering political defeats. But it has certainly also represented a reluctant accommodation by huge numbers of people to the distressing lessons of experience and above all to the realization that it has not after all proved possible, at existing levels of political and economic skill, to combine the range of consumption opportunities open to the majority in advanced capitalist societies with the supposedly egalitarian provision of many aspects of welfare by the modern state. This lesson will stand until it is practically refuted. But even whilst it does stand (which will not necessarily be for very long), it is certainly insufficient in itself to remove the systematic offensiveness to its citizens of life in a capitalist society. Only two sorts of inducements can be expected to lead men and women to put up with this offensiveness: the pressure of their own more or less rational judgements of what will prove for the best and the direct compulsion of force or deprivation. Of these two in any capitalist country in which the state itself remains a democracy it is predominantly the first, opinion, which is decisive. Political compliance and subordination were attributed in eighteenth-century Britain by Adam Smith himself to the natural modesty of mankind.[110] But it seems on the whole more realistic in modern political conditions to ascribe prevailing degrees of political subordination to capitalist requirements to historical despondency rather than to natural modesty.[111] It is just possible that even in a democratic state the majority of the population (those who own little but their labour and own virtually none of the means of production) might come to see socialist expedients through the eyes of Hayek or Mrs Thatcher – as primitive and collectively irrational attempts to interfere with an economic mechanism which it is collectively advantageous to permit to operate with as little interference as possible. But it is very hard indeed, under the pressures of class resentment and in the face of entirely accurate sectional perceptions of short-term advantage, to imagine such a majority sustaining this view, and the devastatingly selective conception of the workings of a capitalist economy on which it depends, for very long.

XXXV.

There are a great many doubts and difficulties about socialist politics which have been resolutely ignored here – most importantly perhaps those concerned with economic, political and military relations between states.[112] Socialism has been considered here simply as an aspect of the domestic politics of modern states. Within this frame a number of judgements have determined the shape of the treatment. Socialist politics, as a form of thought and action involving thousands of millions of human beings, has been a product of powerful and continuing human reasons and motives for at least a century and a half. Like other forms of political agency, socialist politics has proved lamentably prone to self-deception, to the inability to face up to the bad news about its own cognitive and moral limitations. Like any other form of political agency, also, it has been sucked deeply into the machiavellian vortex of violence and fraud by those who have perverted its ideals in the heat of the struggle for political transformation or travestied them shamelessly in the quest for personal power.

To acknowledge these mishaps and deficiencies is not an idle exercise in cultural pessimism. Human beings have always lived in a dangerous world; and, even taken individually and without heavy armaments, they are themselves moderately dangerous creatures: creatures for whom behaving decently, humbly and generously will always be something of a strain and who feel at best ambivalent about the demands placed upon them for mutual restraint and mutual concern. Socialism has sometimes presented itself as a magical recipe for enabling them to behave admirably without strain and for removing the ambivalence from human responsibilities. But it has also presented itself more soberly and honourably as a political project for acting together to refashion human societies (and particularly those produced by industrial capitalism) into a morally more acceptable shape.

It is clear by now (and should no doubt always have been clear) that this refashioning is a very complicated task; that success in it is always likely to be extremely partial. There are perhaps two principal but practically connected difficulties that it presents. The first concerns the organization of production, from the subjective meaning of work, through the patterns and modes of its allocation and sanctioning within a particular population, to the system through which productive activities are concerted. It has proved difficult for the socialist organization of work thus far to improve dramatically[113] on that which obtains in advanced capitalist democracies with strong independent worker organizations.[114] Even more crucially, it has proved extremely difficult in socialist economies to concert productive activities effectively. It seems likely at present that these economies face an inescapable choice between employing a wide variety of market mechanisms (which in practice generate at least quasi-property rights in the means of production and actively encourage the economic competitiveness and the relentless pursuit of personal material advantage so prominent under capitalism) and tolerating in production levels of anarchy and waste which are not markedly (if at all) superior to those which occur in capitalist economies, and, in consumption, a continuation of systematic unconcern for the needs and tastes of those who use the goods and services in question.[115] There are political impediments to improving actual socialist economies (sinister interests and so on) just as there are to improving actual capitalist economies. But the political impediments pale into insignificance before the formidable difficulty of the purely intellectual puzzle of just what expedients can confidently be expected to produce superior effects. It is no easier to solve intellectual problems in a socialist than in a capitalist society and rather less easy even to attempt to do so where the former happens to interfere brutally with freedom of speech and the latter happens to be relatively liberal and democratic. Economics is a very difficult subject and its capacity to guide the practical decisions of rulers for the better is not as yet impressive. Because socialist production depends for its effectiveness upon the precision of human understanding, it can only in principle constitute an improvement over capitalist production where this understanding is powerful and accurate. From this point of view the slow pressure towards socialism within capitalist democracies has given ample opportunity to devise institutions and expedients of a socialist character, to learn to understand their workings and to adapt them in the light of experience so that they work more effectively.

It is perfectly true that these opportunities have arisen within what is in many ways a politically malign ecology and in the face of fierce political opposition. But there is no reason at present to suppose that history has yet offered, or that it will in future offer, more propitious ecological settings for socialist experiment. On the whole, thus far, this opportunity has not been taken very impressively. To take it more impressively in future will require a sharper and more realistic understanding of why existing socialist institutions and expedients have not worked very well (particularly in production) and the provision of cogent reasons why they can be expected to work better in the future. The failures of democratic socialism in the West over the last ten years have been predominantly intellectual failures, failures in comprehension and not in intrepidity or the capacity for evocative non-rational persuasion.

The second principal difficulty in a socialist refashioning of society is one of political organization: not in the narrow design of a political instrument for the appropriation of a power to be magically exerted for the better, but in the far broader issue of what form of political power and organization might actually aid the extension of socialism. It is now reasonably widely acknowledged that the strictly political component of socialist theory has always been a trifle perfunctory.[116] Given the unnerving level of dependence of a socialist society on accuracy and depth of political comprehension this is a dismaying weakness. Here, too, the piecemeal opportunities for institutional experiment and the relatively unfettered opportunities for political reflection and analysis offered by capitalist democracies provide less murky and hazardous conditions for beginning to rectify the deficiency; and the impossibility of making a significant socialist advance without securing the active and comprehending support of a large proportion of the population is more a source of reassurance than a ground for complaint.

The purpose of a socialist society is to express in the structure and texture of their social relations the judgements and sentiments of a human population on how these social relations ought to be. Where the great majority of this population clearly accepts the legitimacy of unrestricted private ownership, this purpose is not merely politically precluded in practice, it is unrealizable (on a socialist view) even in principle. As Stalin memorably showed, economies without private ownership can be inaugurated against the clear desires of the majority of a population. But the purpose of having a socialist society at all cannot be realized except through the judgements and sentiments of its own inhabitants. Their refractoriness and distrust at any given time must simply be taken as a given. It can, and *ex hypothesi* should, be argued against; but it cannot be overridden by the exercise of power. (There could hardly in principle be a rapid and wholly voluntary decision by an entire population to move from capitalism to socialism. But if expropriation is protracted and legal, rather than swift and violent, and if the society is plainly improving for most of its members for most of the period of transition, there is more prospect of alleviating the pains of loss by moral suasion.) The political analogue of the socialist hope that culture can in the end dominate structure and human values govern the organization of production is the hope that this dominance can be secured through the construction and sustaining of a political culture of mutual credibility and goodwill. The charade of belief can be mustered by any capably repressive political order. But the actuality of belief has to be fought for and won incessantly.

Either in a socialist political party competing for political power, or in an incumbent socialist government exercising such power, the central purely political duty which falls upon it is the duty to be credible to those to whom it appeals for its support or over whom it rules. Because the goal of a socialist society is that its members should see and feel their relation to it as an expression of what they themselves truly value, socialist representation, if it is to realize its own objective, must be experienced as voluntary cooperation and not as reluctant or involuntary subordination. The duty to be credible is in the end an intellectual duty. The socialist hope is a deeply rationalist hope (in an impatient and confident form a ludicrously rationalist hope). It requires of its political exponents the capacity to win the trust and support of the majority of a population in terms of their existing beliefs and sentiments and to use such power as it gains in a manner which deserves their trust because its consequences genuinely do serve their interests. It must win their allegiance in their own terms (however cognitively haphazard these may be) and use this allegiance in ways which are objectively to their advantage. The tension between these two demands is often painful. It imposes upon socialist politics an endless educational (and self-educational) task, a struggle to bring the beliefs of politicians and people alike into better conformity with the demands of reality and moral decency. Unsurprisingly, this task is often shirked. Dogmatic leaderships ignore the beliefs and values of the majority and impose their own confident sense of reality's demands, overtly or covertly, upon the supposedly worse judgements of those whom they lead or rule. Cowardly leaderships defer, on the whole overtly, to the manifestly worse judgements of those whom they lead or rule and avert their eyes from the damage which will certainly follow from their actions.

Because this synthesis of subjective and objective credibility is such a formidable and exhausting task, the leaderships of socialist parties in the twentieth century have shown themselves all too eager to elude it. The great advantage of an operating capitalist democracy is that it forces any socialist contender for political power who hopes to exercise this for any length of time at least to attempt this task as a precondition for obtaining power. Because, whilst in operation, it ensures freedom of complaint and the opportunity for subsequent political choice – the two principal requirements for responsible government – capitalist democracy guarantees that movement towards socialism will occur (where it does occur) only insofar as socialist leaderships make themselves, and contrive to remain, credible.

This is not a constraint to which any socialist can defensibly take exception.

XXXVI.

These are not inspiring conclusions.

There is no guarantee that most or all human societies will ever become truly socialist or communist. There is at least equally little guarantee that such human societies as do achieve the public ownership of the means of production will realize any of the more enticing hopes of socialist thinkers. But there is every reason to regard the impetus towards socialism as inseparable from capitalist production and to expect its future, accordingly, to prove at least as protracted as that of the latter. No one has yet devised a politically superior alternative to the patient, tentative and obstructed struggle to transform capitalist democracies for the better through their constitutionally sanctioned political institutions. It is still an open question, still intellectually quite unclear, how far such transformation can benignly go in a socialist direction. How far it will go in practice in a socialist direction will depend very heavily on the answers to this question (though, like all other political outcomes, it will also depend partly on force and fraud and the chaotic interventions of Fortuna). Socialist politics is paralysed at present far more by its massive intellectual failures and its queasy honesty than by any diminution in the repulsiveness of capitalist society. (It is also, of course, a trifle mauled by the at least equal repulsiveness of existing socialist societies.)

XXXVII.

It cannot be said that political theorists have yet had much success in explaining the modern historical trajectories of representative democracy or of socialism. On present showing it appears likely that these two trajectories are closely linked.

The modern democratic capitalist state, it seems, is the natural political expression of a form of society irritably but rationally aware of its own internal contradictions, but also irritably but rationally unconvinced of the possibility of transforming itself into a less contradictory form: a form which contrives to retain its current attractions, which is free of its current blemishes, and yet which possesses no novel blemishes of its own of even greater import. As Groucho Marx is reported once to have observed of sex: it is likely to be with us for some time.

Unless, of course, we contrive instead to exterminate ourselves.

Notes

1 Charles Taylor, 'Political Theory and Practice', in Christopher Lloyd (ed.), *Social Theory and Political Practice*, Oxford University Press, Oxford 1983, 62.

2 Karl Marx, *Capital*, vol. 1, Foreign Languages Publishing House, Moscow 1961, 8–9. 'Intrinsically, it is not a question of the higher or lower degree of development of the social antagonisms that result from the natural laws of capitalist production. It is a question of these laws themselves, of these tendencies working with iron necessity towards inevitable results. The country that is more developed industrially only shows, to the less developed, the image of its own future.' And cf. the article of 31 December 1848, *Neue Rheinische Zeitung*, 'The Revolutionary Movement' (Karl Marx and Frederick Engels, *Collected Works*, vol. 8, Lawrence & Wishart, London 1977, 213–15, esp. 215.

3 Cf. John Harris, 'The Marxist Conception of Violence', *Philosophy and Public Affairs*, III, 2, Winter 1974, 192–220, with Susan James, 'The Duty to Relieve Suffering', *Ethics*, XCIII, 1, October 1982, 4–21.

4 John Dunn (ed.), *West African States: Failure and Promise*, Cambridge University Press, Cambridge 1978, Conclusion.

5 Robert Nozick, *Anarchy, State and Utopia*, Basil Blackwell, Oxford 1975; cf. review, J. Dunn, *Ratio*, XIX, 1, June 1977, 88–95.

6 David Hume, *A Treatise of Human Nature*, J.M. Dent & Son, London 1911, Vol. 2, Bk III, esp. Pt II, sections 1–3: 184–216.

7 F.A. Hayek, *New Studies in Philosophy, Politics, Economics and the History of Ideas*, Routledge & Kegan Paul, London 1978. Cf. John Dunn, 'From Applied Theology to Social Analysis: the break between John Locke and the Scottish Enlightenment', in Istvan Hont and Michael Ignatieff (eds.), *Wealth and Virtue*, Cambridge University Press, Cambridge 1983, 119–35.

8 Cf. Adam Smith, *An Inquiry into the Nature and Causes of the Wealth of Nations*, ed. R.H. Campbell, A.S. Skinner and W.B. Todd, 2 vols., Clarendon Press, Oxford 1976.

9 John Rawls, *A Theory of Justice*, Oxford University Press, Oxford 1972. (And see Michael J. Sandel, *Liberalism and the Limits of Justice*, Cambridge University Press, Cambridge 1982; Ronald Dworkin, 'What is Equality?: Part 1. Equality of Welfare', *Philosophy and Public Affairs*, X, 3, Summer 1981, 185–246; 'What is Equality?: Part 2. Equality of Resources', *Philosophy and Public Affairs*, X, 4, Fall 1981, 283–345.)

10 Rawls, *A Theory of Justice*; Norman Daniels (ed.), *Reading Rawls: Critical Studies of*

a Theory of Justice, Basil Blackwell, Oxford 1975; Nozick, *Anarchy, State and Utopia*; Dworkin, 'What is Equality? Parts 1 and 2' and *Taking Rights Seriously*, Duckworth, London 1977; Bruce Ackerman, *Social Justice in the Liberal State*, Yale University Press, New Haven 1980; and especially Sandel, *Liberalism and the Limits of Justice*. Liberal conceptions of the good have extremely little to do with the way the social, economic or political world today actually is: cf. John Dunn, *Western Political Theory in the Face of the Future*, Cambridge University Press, Cambridge 1979 and 'The Future of Liberalism', University of Guelph, June 1983 (reprinted in John Dunn, *Rethinking Modern Political Theory*, Cambridge University Press, Cambridge, forthcoming).

11 Cf. P.F. Strawson, 'Freedom and Resentment', in Strawson (ed.), *Studies in the Philosophy of Thought and Action*, Oxford University Press, London 1968, 71–96; and, more concretely, Pietro Marcenaro and Vittorio Foa, *Riprendere Tempo*, Giulio Einaudi, Turin 1982.

12 Cf. particularly the positions adopted by Colonel Rainborough in the Putney Debates in 1647 (A.S.P. Woodhouse (ed.), *Puritanism and Liberty*, J.M. Dent & Son, London 1938, 1–124) and by the Abbé Sieyès before the meeting of the Estates-General in 1789 (*What is the Third Estate?*, tr. M. Blondel, Pall Mall Press, London 1963).

13 Sieyès, *What is the Third Estate?*, esp. 104, 177.

14 Nozick, *Anarchy, State and Utopia*, 163 (and 160–4 generally).

15 Dunn, *Ratio*, 1977, 88–95; G.A. Cohen, 'Freedom, Justice and Capitalism', *New Left Review*, 126, March–April 1981, 3–16.

16 Nozick, *Anarchy, State and Utopia*, esp. 178.

17 W.B. Greenleaf, *The British Political Tradition*, vols. 1 and 2, Methuen & Co, London 1983.

18 See George Lichtheim, *The Origins of Socialism*, Frederick Praeger pb. edn, New York 1969; *A Short History of Socialism*, Praeger Publishers, New York 1970; Leszek Kolakowski, *Main Currents of Marxism*, tr. P.S. Falla, 3 vols., Clarendon Press, Oxford 1978. Both Lichtheim and Kolakowski, of course, represent distinctive political points of view and neither is necessarily very fair to the sharply contrasting points of view of which they write.

19 Cf. John Dunn, 'Totalitarian Democracy and the Legacy of Modern Revolutions', *Totalitarian Democracy and After* (Israel Academy of Sciences, Jerusalem 1985. (Reprinted in Dunn, *Rethinking Modern Political Theory*.)

20 Ralph Miliband, *Parliamentary Socialism: A Study in the Politics of Labour*, pb. edn Merlin Press, London 1964, 85 n1.

21 Karl Marx and Frederick Engels, *On Britain*, Foreign Languages Publishing House, Moscow 1953, 499–500.

22 Cf. John Dunn, 'Social Theory, Social Understanding and Political Action', in Lloyd (ed.), *Social Theory and Political Practice*, Oxford University Press, Oxford 1983, 109–35.

23 The most important exploration of this issue is the massive *œuvre* of Jürgen Habermas. It is quite clear, however, that these conditions could not be satisfied in the national politics of any existing society. (Cf. Raymond Geuss, *The Idea of a Critical Theory*, Cambridge University Press, Cambridge 1981.)

24 National problems have no specifically socialist solutions.

25 Ralph Miliband, *Parliamentary Socialism; Capitalist Democracy in Britain*, Oxford University Press, Oxford 1982.

26 F.A. Hayek, *New Studies; Law, Legislation and Liberty*, 3 vols., Routledge & Kegan Paul, London 1973–9 (esp. vol. 2, chaps. 8 and 9).

27 Thomas Babington Macaulay, *The Miscellaneous Writings and Speeches*, Longmans Green, London 1882 esp. 'Mill on Government' (*Edinburgh Review* March 1829), 175–8; Speech on the suffrage, 2 March 1831, 483–92 (esp. 484–5); Speech on the People's Charter, 3 May 1842, 625–6: 'The essence of the Charter is universal suffrage. If you withhold that, it matters not very much what else you grant. If you grant that, it matters not at all what else you withhold. If you grant that, the country is lost . . . My firm conviction is that, in our country, universal suffrage is incompatible, not with this or that form of government, but with all forms of government, and with everything for the sake of which forms of government exist; that it is incompatible with property, and that it is consequently incompatible with civilisation.'

28 André Gorz, *Farewell to the Proletariat: An Essay on Post-Industrial Socialism*, tr. Michael Sonenscher, Pluto Press, London 1982; and for an additional perspective of misjudgement see Tom Nairn, *The Break-up of Britain*, 2nd edn pb. Verso, London 1981 and Benedict Anderson, *Imagined Communities*, New Left Books, London 1983.

29 On the classical republican tradition see particularly J.G.A. Pocock, *The Machiavellian Moment*, Princeton University Press, Princeton 1975.

30 For a powerful account of the degree to which this was true even of ancient participatory democracies see M.I. Finley, *Politics in the Ancient World*, Cambridge University Press, Cambridge 1983.

31 Karl Marx, *The Civil War in France*, in Karl Marx and Frederick Engels, *Selected Works*, Foreign Languages Publishing House, Moscow 1958, vol. 1, 473–545.

32 '. . . apart from the fact that this was merely the rising of a city under exceptional conditions, the majority of the Commune was in no way socialist, nor could it be'. (Letter from Marx to F. Domela-Nieuwenhuis, 22 February 1881, Karl Marx and Frederick Engels, *Selected Correspondence*, Foreign Languages Publishing House, Moscow 1956, 409–11, at 410.) For the context of Marx's response in 1871 see Henry Collins and Chimen Abramsky, *Karl Marx and the British Labour Movement*, Macmillan & Co., London 1965.

33 Cf. John Locke, *Two Treatises of Government*, ed. Peter Laslett, 2nd edn, Cambridge University Press, Cambridge 1967, II, para. 7, 289–90.

34 Cf. Barry Hindess, *The Decline of Working Class Politics*, Paladin, London 1971.

35 Michael Oakeshott, *Rationalism in Politics*, Methuen & Co., London 1962, esp. 1–36, 111–36.

36 The concept of a single-class occupational community is imprecise but potentially illuminating: (Graeme Salaman, *Community and Occupation*, Cambridge University Press, Cambridge 1974).

37 Compare Hal Draper, *Karl Marx's Theory of Revolution*: Pt I. *State and Bureaucracy*, 2 vols., Monthly Review Press, New York 1977 with Alan Gilbert, *Marx's Politics: Communists and Citizens*, Martin Robertson & Co., Oxford 1981.

38 Compare, from very different angles, Gorz, *Farewell to the Proletariat*; Alec Nove,

The Economics of Feasible Socialism, George Allen & Unwin, London 1982; Michael Ellman, *Socialist Planning*, Cambridge University Press, Cambridge 1979.

39 Albert Hirschman, *Exit, Voice and Loyalty: responses to decline in firms, organizations and states*, Harvard University Press, Cambridge, Mass. 1970, 79 '. . . the most loyalist behavior retains an enormous dose of reasoned calculation'. But cf. the whole of chapter 7, 'A Theory of Loyalty', in which loyalty is conceived as a slightly equivocal maximizing strategy, involving a considerable variety of trade-offs.

40 Niccolò Machiavelli, *Il Principe*, chaps. 15–19 (in Machiavelli, *Tutte le Opere*, ed. Mario Martelli, G.C. Sansoni, Florence 1971, 280–91).

41 Cf. John Dunn, *Locke*, Oxford University Press, Oxford 1984; and 'Trust in the Political Theory of John Locke' in Richard Rorty, J.B. Schneewind and Quentin Skinner (eds.), *Philosophy in History*, Cambridge University Press, Cambridge 1984.

42 V.I. Lenin, *What is to be Done?*, in V.I. Lenin, *Selected Works*, 2 vols., Foreign Languages Publishing House, Moscow 1947, vol. 1, 145–269; Neil Harding, *Lenin's Political Thought*, vol. 1, Macmillan & Co., London 1977, chaps. 5–7.

43 Cf. *Vladimir Akimov on the Dilemmas of Russian Marxism 1895–1903*, tr. and ed. Jonathan Frankel, Cambridge University Press, Cambridge 1969.

44 Compare, for example, Barrington Moore Jr, *Injustice: The Social Bases of Obedience and Revolt*, M.E. Sharpe, White Plains, New York 1978; Antony Giddens, *The Class Structure of the Advanced Societies*, Hutchinson & Co., London 1973.

45 Carl von Clausewitz, *On War*, ed. & tr. Michael Howard and Peter Paret, Princeton University Press, Princeton, NJ 1976, bk 1, chap 7, 'Friction in War', 119–21.

46 See Nove, *Economics of Feasible Socialism*, and, particularly, Ellman, *Socialist Planning*.

47 And indeed some of his recent commentators (cf. Peter Singer, *Marx*, Oxford University Press, Oxford 1980, esp. 69–73).

48 Cf. Dunn, *Western Political Theory*, chap. 1.

49 'The lust for destruction is also a creative lust.' Michael Bakunin, 'The Reaction in Germany' (1842), *Selected Writings*, ed. Arthur Lehning, Jonathan Cape, London 1973, 58. (I have taken the translation from Lichtheim, *Short History of Socialism*, 124, for reasons expressed there.)

50 Leon Trotsky, *Literature and Revolution*, University of Michigan Press, Ann Arbor 1960, 256: 'Man will become immeasurably stronger, wiser and subtler; his body will become more harmonized, his movements more rhythmic, his voice more musical. The forms of life will become dynamically dramatic. The average human type will rise to the heights of an Aristotle, a Goethe, or a Marx. And above this ridge new peaks will rise.' Cf. Laurence L. Bongie, *David Hume Prophet of the Counter-Revolution*, Clarendon Press, Oxford 1965, 86: Citoyen Carra ('Tout est neuf dans notre révolution') with Citoyen Bancal ('. . . oui, tout est neuf excepté les hommes, qui sont les éléments des révolutions, et qui sont sujets à des passions dans tous les pays et dans tous les siècles') at the debate in the Convention on the trial of Louis XVI.

51 Nove, *Feasible Socialism*, 111.
52 Theda Skocpol, *States and Social Revolutions*, Cambridge University Press, Cambridge 1979.
53 John Dunn, 'Understanding Revolutions', *Ethics*, XCII, 2, January 1982, 299–315.
54 John Dunn, *Modern Revolutions: an Introduction to the Analysis of a Political Phenomenon*, Cambridge University Press, Cambridge 1972.
55 Rawls, *A Theory of Justice*, section 80, 'The Problem of Envy', esp. 530. And cf. Ted Honderich, 'The Question of Well-being and the Principle of Equality', *Mind*, XC, 4, 1981, 481–504, esp. 496–7.
56 Peter Nettl, 'The German Social Democratic Party 1890–1914 as a Political Model', *Past and Present*, 30, April 1965, 65–95; Guenther Roth, *The Social Democrats in Imperial Germany*, Bedminster Press, Totowa, NJ 1963; Carl E. Schorske, *German Social Democracy 1905–1917*, Harper & Row, New York 1972; Peter Gay, *The Dilemma of Democratic Socialism*, Collier Books, New York 1962; Massimo Salvadori, *Karl Kautsky and the Socialist Revolution 1880–1938*, tr. J. Rothschild, New Left Books, London 1979; A.J. Ryder, *The German Revolution of 1918*, Cambridge University Press, Cambridge 1967; and cf. Dick Geary, *European Labour Protest 1848–1939*, Croom Helm, London 1981.
57 Ellman, *Socialist Planning*, chap. 10, 246–76.
58 Dunn, *Western Political Theory*, chap. 1.
59 Ellman, *Socialist Planning*, 265. For the context of the decision see Robert Service, *The Bolshevik Party in Revolution; A Study in Organizational Change 1917–1923*, Macmillan & Co., London 1979, chap. 6, esp. 152–8.
60 Gilbert, *Marx's Politics*; Draper, *Karl Marx's Theory of Revolution*; George Lichtheim, *Marxism: An Historical and Critical Study*, Routledge & Kegan Paul, London 1961; R.N. Hunt, *The Political Ideas of Marx and Engels*, vol. 1, Macmillan & Co., London 1975.
61 Moshe Lewin, *Lenin's Last Struggle*, tr. A.M. Sheridan-Smith, Pluto Press, London 1975; *Political Undercurrents in Soviet Economic Debates*, Pluto Press, London 1975; Neil Harding, *Lenin's Political Thought*, vols. 1 and 2, Macmillan & Co., London 1977–81.
62 Machiavelli, *Il Principe* (*Tutte le Opere*, 284): 'A uno principe, adunque, non è necessario avere in fatto tutte le soprascritte qualità, ma è bene necessario parere di averle.'
63 Nove, *Economics of Feasible Socialism*, strongly emphasizes the intractability of this difficulty in socialist planning.
64 Cf. Gorz, *Farewell to the Proletariat*. But cf. the far more nuanced observations of Marcenaro and Foa, *Riprendere Tempo*, esp. 55.
65 Apart, that is to say, from the threat of external military or nuclear assault, however acute this risk should be judged.
66 Ellman, *Socialist Planning*; Tamás Bauer, 'Investment Cycles in Planned Economies', *Acta Oeconomica*, XXI, 1978, 243–60; Janos Kornai, *Economics of Shortage*, 2 vols., North-Holland, Amsterdam 1980, esp. vol. 2, 569–71; Wlodzimierz Brus, 'East European Economies Facing the Eighties', Afterword to Brus, *The Economic History of Communist Eastern Europe*, Oxford University Press, Oxford 1984.

67 Ellman, *Socialist Planning*, 216—20; and chap. 10.

68 Cf. W.G. Runciman, *Relative Deprivation and Social Justice*, Routledge & Kegan Paul, London 1966.

69 Ellman, *Socialist Planning*, 151.

70 But cf. Stephen Castles and Godula Kosack, *Immigrant Workers and Class Structure in Western Europe*, Oxford University Press, London 1973.

71 National problems are certainly another.

72 Richard M. Titmuss, *The Gift Relationship: From Human Blood to Social Policy*, Penguin Books, Harmondsworth 1973; and cf. Kenneth J. Arrow, 'Gifts and Exchanges', *Philosophy and Public Affairs*, I, 4, Summer 1972, 343—62.

73 Karl Marx, *The German Ideology* (Marx and Engels, *Collected Works*, vol. 5), Lawrence & Wishart, London 1976, 54.

74 Cf. Dunn, 'From Applied Theology to Social Analysis'.

75 Ellman, *Socialist Planning*, 216; Peter Wiles, *Distribution of Income: East and West*, De Vries Lectures, North-Holland, Amsterdam 1974, 104.

76 Miliband, *Capitalist Democracy in Britain*, chap. 6, esp. 155.

77 Norberto Bobbio, *Quale Socialismo? discussione di un alternativa*, Giulio Einaudi, Turin 1976.

78 Antonio Gramsci, *Selections from the Prison Notebooks*, ed. and tr. Q. Hoare and G. Nowell Smith, Lawrence & Wishart, London 1971, 12—13, 53—60, 104—6, 180—2, 238—43, 261—4, 270—6, 416—18; and see Perry Anderson, 'The Antinomies of Antonio Gramsci', *New Left Review*, 100, November 1976, 5—78; Joseph V. Femia, *Gramsci's Political Thought: Hegemony, Consciousness and the Revolutionary Process*, Clarendon Press, Oxford 1981.

79 David Hume, 'Of the First Principles of Government' (1741) in Hume, *Essays Moral, Political and Literary*, Henry Frowde, London 1903, 29—34, esp. 29: 'Nothing appears more surprising to those who consider human affairs with a philosophical eye, than the easiness with which the many are governed by the few; and the implicit submission, with which men resign their own sentiments and passions to those of their rulers. When we inquire by what means this wonder is effected, we shall find, that, as Force is always on the side of the governed, the governors have nothing to support them but opinion. It is, therefore, on opinion only that government is founded.'

80 It is hard to overemphasize the importance in political explanation of the fact that all participants enjoy the opportunity to learn from the experience of political competition. Cf. Dunn, 'Understanding Revolutions' and *Political Obligation in its Historical Context*, Cambridge University Press, Cambridge 1980, chap. 9.

81 Woodhouse (ed.), *Puritanism and Liberty*, 53.

82 Dunn, *Western Political Theory*, chap. 1; Finley, *Politics in the Ancient World* and *Democracy Ancient and Modern*, Rutgers University Press, New Brunswick, NJ 1973.

83 Cf. Quentin Skinner, 'The Idea of a Cultural Lexicon', *Essays in Criticism*, XXIX, 3, July 1979, 205—24; 'Some Problems in the Analysis of Political Thought and Action', *Political Theory*, II, 1974, 277—303.

84 Cf. Nozick, *Anarchy, State and Utopia*.

85 Cf. John Dunn and A.F. Robertson, *Dependence and Opportunity: Political Change*

in Ahafo, Cambridge University Press, Cambridge 1973, chap. 4 and esp. 167–8.

86 Georg Lukács, *History and Class Consciousness*, tr. R. Livingstone, Merlin Press, London 1971 and *Lenin: A Study on the Unity of His Thought*, tr. N. Jacobs, New Left Books, London 1970; and cf. the character Naphta in Thomas Mann, *The Magic Mountain*, tr. H.T. Lowe-Porter, Penguin Books, Harmondsworth 1960.

87 Rawls, *A Theory of Justice*.

88 Nozick, *Anarchy, State and Utopia*; possibly also of aspects of pre-capitalist ideologies (cf. Brian Barry, *The Liberal Idea of Justice*, Clarendon Press, Oxford 1973, esp. 167; David Miller, *Social Justice*, Clarendon Press, Oxford 1976, esp. chap. 8).

89 This is not to say that his theory necessarily gives a very compelling account of how we should in fact conceive social justice. (Cf. Sandel, *Liberalism and the Limits of Justice*.)

90 Adam Smith, *Wealth of Nations*, esp. vol. 1, 456; (and see Donald Winch, *Adam Smith's Politics: An Essay in Historiographic Revision*, Cambridge University Press, Cambridge 1978 and the introduction to Hont and Ignatieff (eds.), *Wealth and Virtue*); Hayek, *New Studies* and *Law, Legislation and Liberty*; Nozick, *Anarchy, State and Utopia*.

91 Auguste Blanqui, interview with *The Times* (London), 27 April 1879 (Alan B. Spitzer, *The Revolutionary Theories of Louis Auguste Blanqui*, Columbia University Press, New York 1957, 135).

92 Cf. Sandel, *Liberalism and the Limits of Justice*; Dunn, *Western Political Theory*; *Political Obligation*, chap. 10 and 'The Future of Liberalism'.

93 J.W. Goethe, *Italian Journey*, tr. W. Auden and E. Mayer, Penguin Books, Harmondsworth 1970, 316–17: 'I am eagerly looking forward to reading the third part of Herder's book . . . I'm sure he will have set forth very well the beautiful dream-wish of mankind that things will be better some day. Speaking for myself, I too believe that humanity will win in the long run; I am only afraid that at the same time the world will have turned into one huge hospital where everyone is everybody else's humane nurse.'

94 Cf. Leszek Kolakowski in Kolakowski & Stuart Hampshire (eds.), *The Socialist Idea: a Reappraisal*, Weidenfeld & Nicolson, London 1974, chaps. 1 and 2.

95 Robert Conquest, *The Great Terror*, Penguin Books, Harmondsworth 1971; François Ponchaud, *Cambodia Year Zero*, Penguin Books, Harmondsworth 1978.

96 See Karl Marx, 'On the Jewish Question' and 'Critical Notes on the Article, "The King of Prussia and Social Reform"', Marx and Engels, *Collected Works*, vol. 3, London 1975, esp. 162–8, 197–9; G. Plekhanov, *Selected Philosophical Works*, vol. 1, Foreign Languages Publishing House, Moscow 1961: 'Socialism and the Political Struggle' (October 1883), 109–16; 'Our Differences' (July 1884), esp. 342–59, 371–2. And see Samuel H. Baron, *Plekhanov: The Father of Russian Marxism*, Stanford University Press, Stanford, Calif. 1963, 358–61 on his vision of the implications of October 1917 itself (and esp. 360, his 1904 criticism of Lenin's organizational approach that, if the Central Committee acquired the right of expulsion from the party, 'we would then have realised the ideal of the Persian Shah').

97 But cf. Geuss, *The Idea of a Critical Theory*; Dunn, *Political Obligation*, chap. 10.

98 Adam Smith, *The Theory of Moral Sentiments*, ed. D.D. Raphael and A.L. Macfie, Clarendon Press, Oxford 1976, 234.

99 Albert Soboul, *The Parisian Sans-Culottes and the French Revolution 1793–94*, tr. Gwynne Lewis, Clarendon Press, Oxford 1964, 140.

100 This is one of the great themes of Marcel Proust, *Remembrance of Things Past*, tr. C.K. Scott Moncrieff and Terence Kilmartin, 3 vols., Penguin Books, Harmondsworth 1983. Cf. e.g. vol. 2, 209 on M. Legrandin: 'For the fact of the matter is that, since we are determined always to keep our feelings to ourselves, we have never given any thought to the manner in which we should express them. And suddenly there is within us a strange and obscene animal making itself heard, whose tones may inspire as much alarm in the person who receives the involuntary, elliptical and almost irresistible communication of one's defect or vice as would the sudden avowal indirectly and outlandishly proffered by a criminal who can no longer refrain from confessing to a murder of which one had never imagined him to be guilty' and the scene between the Guermantes and their intimate friend of several decades, the dying Swann, vol. 2, 618: '"But whatever I do I mustn't make you late; you're dining out, remember"', he added, because he knew that for other people their own social obligations took precedence over the death of a friend, and he put himself in their place thanks to his instinctive politeness. But that of the Duchess enabled her also to perceive in a vague way that the dinner party to which she was going must count for less to Swann than his own death.'

101 Dunn, 'Totalitarian Democracy and the Legacy of Modern Revolutions'.

102 See particularly Kornai, *Economics of Shortage*; Ellman, *Socialist Planning*.

103 A.C. Sutton, *Western Technology and Soviet Economic Development 1917 to 1930*, Hoover Institution Publications, Stanford 1968; *Western Technology and Soviet Economic Development 1930 to 1945*, Hoover Inst., Stanford 1971; *Western Technology and Soviet Economic Development 1945 to 1965*, Hoover Inst., Stanford 1973; but cf. Ellman, *Socialist Planning*, 51–3.

104 Cf. W. Brus: 'Any economy must be coordinated somehow.' (Hillel Ticktin and Wlodomierz Brus, 'Is Market Socialism Possible or Necessary?', *Critique*, 14, 1981, 13–26, 32–9, at 25.)

105 Nozick, *Anarchy, State and Utopia*.

106 Nove, *Economics of Feasible Socialism*.

107 And cf. Amartya Sen and Bernard Williams (eds.), *Utilitarianism and Beyond*, Cambridge University Press, Cambridge 1982, Introduction, 1–21.

108 See e.g., Mike Davis, 'Why the American Working Class is Different', *New Left Review*, 123, Sept.–Oct. 1980, 3–44; 'The Barren Marriage of American Labour', *New Left Review*, 124, Nov.–Dec. 1980, 43–84.

109 Cf. Suzanne Berger (ed.), *Organizing Interests in Western Europe: Pluralism, Corporatism and the Transformation of Politics*, Cambridge University Press, Cambridge 1981, esp. chaps. by Sabel, Offe and Pizzorno.

110 Adam Smith, *Lectures on Jurisprudence*, ed. R.L. Meek, D.D. Raphael and P.G. Stein, Clarendon Press, Oxford 1978, 318.

111 Cf. Barrington Moore Jr, *Injustice*.

112 Cf. John Dunn, 'Unimagined Community: the Deceptions of Socialist Internationalism', Instituto Gramsci, Florence October 1983 (reprinted in

Dunn, *Rethinking Modern Political Theory*).

113 Cf., for example, Ellman, *Socialist Planning*, 157, 164, 169–73, 219; and article by Jean-Claude Chesnais in *La Recherche*, reported in *Sunday Times* (London), 25 September 1983, indicating a fall in male life expectancy in the USSR by over four years since the year 1965.

114 Cf. Steve Tolliday and Jonathan Zeitlin (eds.), *Shop-Floor Bargaining and the State: Historical and Comparative Perspectives*, Cambridge University Press, Cambridge 1984.

115 Nove, *Economics of Feasible Socialism*; and cf. Ellman, *Socialist Planning*, 210.

116 Cf. Bobbio, *Quale Socialismo?*; Ralph Miliband, *Marxism and Politics*, Oxford University Press, Oxford 1977.

Index

Index

Index